A GOOD HEALTH GUIDE

D1347792

How to Relieve
the Pain
of Arthritis

Anne Charlish

How to Relieve the Pain of Arthritis
Anne Charlish

Copyright © MMII The Windsor Group

Published MMII by The Windsor Group,
158 Moulsham Street,
Chelmsford,
Essex CM2 0LD

Type set by SJ De sign and Pub lishing, Bromley, Kent

ISBN 1-903904-03-X

Contents

Introduction

Arthritis may sound to some people as if the joints are a bit stiff and perhaps a little knobbly. But arthritis means a lot more than that to the many thousands of sufferers from this disabling condition.

Arthritis can mean fatigue, stress, daily pain, immobility, inflammation and frustration at not being able to do all the things that one used to do before the disorder crept up on us. There are some 200 different types of arthritis (as you will see in *Chapter 1*) and many different drugs. This book is designed to answer all your questions and to offer you the very latest news on medication and on all the aids and gadgets that will help you in daily life.

Mobility and medication are the two big issues in arthritis: mobility gives us our independence and the right medication soothes inflammation and reduces pain. If one drug doesn't suit you, be sure to ask your doctor to try you on a different drug.

Hip replacements are THE big success story of our time for arthritis sufferers. Joint replacements, such as hip and knee, are described in *Part IV.*

I have written this book for all arthritis sufferers everywhere, young and old alike. You will find that there is a lot of scope for improving your quality of life very greatly: look particularly at *Part II* and *Chapter 25* in *Part IV.*

Anne Charlish
Sussex, 2001

Part I: Finding Out About Arthritis

Chapter 1

What is Arthritis?

Arthritis is defined as pain, stiffness or swelling in or around one of the joints of the body for more than two weeks. The body's skeletal structure is operated by complex interacting sets of muscles, joints and ligaments. The principal joints of the body are the knee joint, the elbow joint, the hip joint and the joints of the hands and feet. Arthritis may develop in any one, or more, of these joints.

The human body comprises over 200 joints. A human joint is a complicated and delicately balanced piece of engineering composed of several components acting together with one another. Because different forms of arthritis produce different sets of symptoms, and also demand different treatments, it helps to understand something of how the body's joints work and what can go wrong, resulting in pain, stiffness or swelling.

A joint is the point at which the bones meet and move against each other.

The body's skeleton is a jointed framework that supports the body and enables it to perform a fantastic range of movements, swift and powerful, fine and delicate, twisting, leaping, bending and lifting. All these movements are controlled by muscles, tendons and ligaments attached to the bones, which can, in this way, be rearranged in relation to one another to accomplish a wide range of actions and positions – such as stretching well above the head, for example, to reach a high cupboard, crouching beneath a table to clean the floor. Where the ends of the bones move against one another, they are cushioned by a layer of cartilage and fluid.

The entire joint is encased in a capsule or sheath which is rich with nerve endings which communicate with the brain. This is why it is so painful when joints are damaged or inflamed. Outside this capsule or sheath the ligaments act to stabilise the joint: they hold it in position and limit the range of the joint.

There are little pads located between the muscle and the joint capsule known as bursae. These act like shock-absorbers to cushion the joint from the stress of sudden and unaccustomed or strong movement, such as jumping, kicking, lifting heavy weights. The bursae become swollen and inflamed under excessive use or pressure and lend the name, bursitis, to a group of occupationally-related forms of arthritis, such as Tennis Elbow.

Given that there are over 200 joints in the human body and over 200 types of arthritis, it is not difficult to see why arthritis is such a common and well-known condition.

The word arthritis means literally inflamed joint. However, the term arthritis does not necessarily or exclusively indicate inflammation of a joint. Arthritis may refer to a joint that is injured, strained, infected or inflamed. When any of the body's joints are affected by arthritis, we suffer discomfort and pain as a result of the nerves in the joint sending messages to the brain.

The smooth interaction between the elements of a joint starts to break down in an unhealthy or ageing joint. In osteoarthritis, for example, the cartilage becomes thin and flaky and begins to split. The bone underneath becomes thicker and eventually starts to project at the edges of the joint almost as if it were trying to reduce the potential degree of movement. The amount of fluid in the joint increases, leading to swelling, stiffness and pain. The capsule that encases the joint is stretched. In severe osteoarthritis the cartilage may wear away completely exposing the bone underneath. Chalky deposits of crystals may form in it which can break off and float around in the fluid. The joint may become permanently deformed.

In rheumatoid arthritis inflammation starts in the membrane surrounding the joint (the synovium), which then thickens and begins to occupy the space within the joint. The inflammation spreads to the rest of the joint capsule, and the ligaments and tendons that surround and support it become stretched so that the joint may become unstable. If the inflammation remains unchecked the cartilage in the joint will shrink and the exposed ends of the bone become eaten away leading to still further deformation.

The joints of the body vary considerably in their structure. Some, like the hip, are more flexible than others with all round rotation. The elbow, on the other hand, moves only backward and forward. In the spine the interconnected vertebrae have even less independent movement and they are jointed without a capsule or any lubricating fluid. This leaves the disc of cushioning cartilage between them with an even more crucial role to play and contributes to back pain being the most widespread and intractable form of joint pain.

TYPES OF ARTHRITIS

There are well over 200 types of arthritis. The most common of these are osteoarthritis, rheumatoid arthritis, and gout. Some less common types of arthritis are also described. Arthritis types can be classified as follows:

1. Wear and tear

Degenerative arthritis includes the most common type of arthritis, osteoarthritis. Joints, just like the moving parts of any machine, wear out and perform less reliably with heavy use and with the passage of time. Joints of the human body simply wear out. You may get arthritis as you become older because your cartilage is the type that becomes thin and flaky with age, or because you have subjected your joints to very heavy use on the sports field or imposed excessive strain upon them by loading them with too much body weight. It is possible that one of your hip joints is subjected to excessive wear through one of your legs being longer than the other. This is not uncommon.

2.   Inflammation

In inflammatory types of arthritis, of which the most common type is rheumatoid arthritis, the cause of the inflammation is unknown. Ankylosing spondylitis is another form of inflammatory arthritis.

3.   Breakdown in body chemistry

The most common of these diseases is gout, in which the joint becomes inflamed because the body fails to break down harmful crystals or uric acid which form inside the joint, causing intense pain.

Some types of arthritis are a combination of both inflammation and wear and tear. Arthritis can also be caused by bacterial infection (septic arthritis).

WHAT IS RHEUMATISM?

Rheumatism is a generally understood term to describe aches and pains in the muscles or joints, often those aches caused by a damp, wintry atmosphere. It is not a recognised medical term. Healthcare professionals use the following classifications: rheumatic diseases, rheumatic disorders or disorders of the musculoskeletal system.

OSTEOARTHRITIS

Osteoarthritis (OA) is the most common form of arthritis. It most often affects middle-aged and older people. The sites usually affected are the neck, lower back, knees, hips and joints of the fingers. The big toe is often affected by osteoarthritis, but problems with the big toe should not be confused with gout.

Nearly 70 per cent of people over the age of 70 have X-ray evidence of OA. However, only half of these people develop symptoms of the disease. OA may also occur in joints that have been previously injured, been subjected to prolonged heavy use, or damaged by prior infection or inflammatory arthritis. People with OA experience pain and loss of function of the affected joints.

Osteoarthritis results from the gradual degeneration of the cartilage that surrounds and cushions the affected joint. Healthy cartilage that covers the end of the bone in the joint is normally very smooth, strong and flexible. In OA this gradually becomes pitted, rough and brittle. The causes of cartilage loss are multiple.

The thin layer of cartilage at the end the bones acts as a shock-absorber and helps the joint to move. The bone end and cartilage are surrounded by a membrane called the synovium. As the cartilage at the end of the bones wears away, the bone beneath thickens and grows outwards, thus enlarging the joint. It can also form spurs at the edges of the joint – these are known as osteophytes. These spurs are partly responsible for the very bony, gnarled and twisted appearance of hands that you sometimes see in older people who suffer with the disease.

Osteoarthritis is a slow disease which may take many, many years to develop. In some people it produces little more than stiffness, while in others the disease can cause considerable discomfort and disability. Some kinds of OA are known to be hereditary, including the common form causing enlargement of the knuckles where a specific genetic abnormality has been found.

It is important if you suspect that you may be suffering with OA to consult your doctor in order that a firm diagnosis may be made.

The chief signs and symptoms are as follows:

☐ In the early stages of the disease, the sufferer will experience pain after using the joint and the pain may become worse as the day progresses.

☐ In the later stages, the joint may become painful with even minimal movement, at rest and during the night.

☐ Stiffness of the joints is usually confined to a local area and lasts for only a short time.

☐ There may also be some tenderness in the area of the affected joint.

To begin with the pain, stiffness and restriction of movement that OA causes will only bother you occasionally and will get better with rest. The joint may become noisy, creaking, clicking or crunching – this is known as crepitation. This happens because the cartilage that cushions the bone inside the joint roughens with wear and tear and no longer moves as smoothly and silently as before. You will probably find that your symptoms come and go. Damp weather may aggravate your condition, as may exercise. You may notice some swelling which may be bony (in a big toe joint, for example) or fluid (seen in the knees and ankles).

The joints most commonly affected are:

☐ The hands.

☐ The knees (with which you may experience pain and tenderness).

☐ The hips (you may experience pain in the groin or inner thigh and you may also experience what is known as referred pain in the buttocks, the sciatic region or the knee. You may find that movement of the hip now becomes limited, particularly the rotating movement).

☐ The feet (especially the big toe).

☐ The spine (most commonly the lower back, but the vertebrae of the neck may also be affected).

RHEUMATOID ARTHRITIS

Rheumatoid arthritis (RA) is the commonest form of arthritis after osteoarthritis. RA affects five times more women than men and it usually starts between the ages of 25 to 50. RA is not a degenerative, wear and tear disorder like osteoarthritis. It is an inflammatory autoimmune disease that affects the joints.

The inflammation starts in the synovium (lining of the joint), but this leads to the release of painful substances into the joint space causing swelling or effusion and damage to the bone (erosion). There may also be inflammation of the tendons (tenosynovitis) and effects on the sufferer's general sense of well-being. The main symptoms are joint pain and stiffness. Other symptoms include swelling in the joints, lack of appetite, low grade fever, extreme fatigue and lumps under the skin around the elbows and fingers.

The cause of RA is not known. It is a much more distressing and troublesome condition than OA both in the short and long term. It can strike at any age, including childhood (see JRA), but it starts most frequently in youth or middle age. RA affects all races and all climes but the disease tends to be more severe in northern Europe than in other parts of the world.

People who contract RA may have a single acute attack that persists for several months, or longer, but which then clears up and never reappears. Or, the disease may continue for the rest of their life, when it becomes chronic. Only in a minority of cases does the disease persist to the point of becoming severely crippling.

There may be pain and tenderness in the bases of the toes (but not in the big toe, unlike gout) and swelling of joints. The joints most commonly affected are those of the hands, arms and legs. It usually but not invariably affects both sides symmetrically. RA can affect the jaw occasionally and, rarely, the spine.

RA can cause inflammation of other organs of the body as well, including the glands of the eyes and mouth, the blood vessels, and the outer lining of the heart and lungs. Severe RA can cause permanent damage to the body tissue and cartilage of the joints and it can eventually deform and even destroy the joint.

There is considerable variation from one person to another in how RA manifests itself. Sometimes only one or two joints are affected. In other people, the disease is widespread and very active. About 30 per cent of people who contract RA appear to recover completely within a few years. About 65 per cent continue to suffer pains in their joints, swellings and sudden flare-ups, while around 5 per cent become severely affected and extensively disabled.

If you suspect that you have contracted RA, you should consult your doctor without delay. Confirmation of diagnosis is made through X-rays and blood tests which can detect the presence of inflammation.

The American College of Rheumatology uses the following criteria to establish a positive diagnosis:

- ☐ The presence of arthritis for longer than six weeks.
- ☐ Prolonged morning stiffness in the joints.
- ☐ Presence of characteristic nodules under the skin.
- ☐ Joint erosions apparent on X-ray.
- ☐ Positive blood tests of an antibody known as rheumatoid factor.

However, 25 per cent of people with RA never develop this factor. This antibody may also be present in people who do not have RA.

Normally, referral to a consultant rheumatologist follows a positive diagnosis by a family doctor.

There is no need to respond to a diagnosis of RA with despair. Most people experience the disease in its mild form. Even in those people who have severe RA, some find that they get dramatically better – for no apparent reason. Although RA is a chronic disease, a sufferer may experience long periods of time with no symptoms. Absence of symptoms, or remission, can last days, months or even years.

JUVENILE ARTHRITIS

Arthritis affects 1 in 1,000 children every year. People tend to think of arthritis as an older person's disease, and there may therefore be some delay in diagnosing arthritis in a child. The majority of children with arthritis have what is known as acute reactive arthritis following a viral or bacterial infection. This type usually clears up within a few weeks or months.

Juvenile rheumatoid arthritis (JRA) is the most common type of arthritis that persists for months or years.

GOUT

Gout is caused by uric acid crystals in the joints. We all produce uric acid, normally in amounts that the body can cope with. Uric acid is a substance that is formed when the body breaks down waste products. It is normally excreted in the urine. If there is an excess of uric acid produced in the body, it accumulates and crystals form. These crystals form in and around the joints of the body. If the crystals enter the joint space they cause inflammation, swelling and severe pain.

Gout commonly attacks the joint of the big toe but it may also affect other joints, the ankles, knees, hands, wrists or elbows. It can also affect the skin of the ears and the hands, causing swelling.

The affected joint starts to ache, then quickly becomes swollen, red, very warm and extremely painful. The attack usually lasts for a few days, then dies down, and the joint gradually returns to normal.

Gout is essentially a defect in the body's internal chemistry. It affects four times as many men as women. When gout affects women, it usually does so after the menopause when they have less natural protection against the disease. Gout is a very controllable (although not curable) disease, but if left untreated it can cause crippling arthritis, raised blood pressure and kidney disease which may eventually prove fatal.

Some people are more susceptible to gout than others. In those people who already have a predisposition, triggers for gout include too much high-protein food, alcohol (not only port), infections, injury, antibiotics, diuretics, aspirin, crash diets. Some people find that red meat and alcohol (including red wine, port, beer, brandy, whisky) can trigger an attack.

There are three approaches to treatment for gout. The first is treatment for the pain. The second is treatment for the inflammation in which anti-inflammatory drugs are used. You are advised to take plenty of rest, to increase your fluid intake, especially water, and to cut down on red meats and alcohol. The third treatment involves a combination of drugs, which you will have to take for the rest of your life. The first drug increases the excretion of uric acid via the kidneys (and you must of course also increase your intake of fluids) and the second drug reduces the amount of acid produced by the body in the first place.

It is most important to remember to take no painkillers if you suspect you have gout, except those prescribed by your doctor. Aspirin, for example, can actually slow down the excretion of uric acid from the body, thereby aggravating the disease.

PSEUDO GOUT

Pseudo gout is a form of arthritis caused by deposits of calcium crystals in the joints of the body rather than uric acid crystals as in gout. The term pseudo gout refers to the gout-like attacks of joint inflammation that occur in many people suffering from this condition. The calcium containing crystal deposits that are found in the cartilage of the joints may be visible on X-rays of the affected joint.

Acute attacks of pseudo gout often occur in the knee joints and can incapacitate the sufferer for weeks. Pseudo gout is not as hazardous as gout in that it is a relatively harmless disease unless the crystals become dislodged, in which case they can also set up inflammation in the joint, less painful than in gout, which is usually treated by anti-inflammatory drugs or by drawing off the fluid containing the crystals with a syringe. Only if the swelling and inflammation are neglected can the disease cause long-term damage.

Pseudo gout, like gout, is controllable but not curable. It is important that correct diagnosis is made as it can be confused with gout (which can lead to RA) and because, like gout, the treatment for pseudo gout is specific.

ANKYLOSING SPONDYLITIS

This is a relatively uncommon form of arthritis, affecting approximately 1 person in 1,000. Ankylosing spondylitis (AS) is a painful, progressive, rheumatic disease of the vertebrae of the spine. As a result of the inflammation, scar tissue forms in the space between the vertebrae, making the joint stiff. This tissue may turn to bone. So, when the inflammation dies down, it leaves bony deposits on the rim of the inflamed vertebrae. Bone has grown out from either side of the affected vertebrae and may eventually grow together. There is a danger that these eventually fuse into one continuous bone, producing a rigid poker spine.

AS affects many more men than women, to the ratio of about 2.5:1. Young men usually contract the disease between the ages of 17 and 27, typically in their early twenties. The cause is not known, but there is a genetic inheritance factor. However, not all those people who carry the gene go on to develop the full-blown disease.

AS starts with persistent back pain and a characteristic early morning stiffness which tends to become easier with movement during the day. This is what differentiates AS from other back pains, which tend to become worse during the day rather than better.

Other symptoms of AS include chronic fatigue, losing weight and pain in other parts of the body. There may be pain in the chest and ribs, making it difficult to breathe. There may also be pain in the buttocks and the backs of the thighs. The ankles may become swollen and the heel bones tender. The bone at the base of the spine will be painful.

It is important to go to the doctor if you suspect that you are suffering with AS in order that the condition can be treated promptly. If it is not treated, the spine may stiffen as described above. Blood tests and X-rays are used to make a definitive diagnosis.

The relief of AS depends on mobility and warmth. Swimming is useful for improving mobility as is running. Contact sports are not recommended as there is a higher risk of injury with these. Hot baths, hot-water bottles or an electric blanket together with a firm bed will prove helpful. When you are working, change your position frequently so that you are not holding your spine in one fixed position for long periods.

One of the complications of AS, a relatively rare one, is iritis or uveitis. The symptoms are red, painful eyes and you should attend the Accident & Emergency department of your local hospital without delay if you experience this in order to prevent any permanent damage.

AS is one of a group of inflammatory forms of arthritis, known collectively as seronegative arthritis because the distinctive rheumatoid antibody, the marker of RA, is not found in the blood serum of patients with these diseases. Other seronegative forms of arthritis include reactive arthritis, Reiter's disease, psoriatic and colitic arthritis in which arthritis may follow an infection. The infections themselves may be mild or almost without symptoms, so that special medical investigations are needed to show the cause of the arthritis.

LESS COMMON TYPES OF ARTHRITIS

Systemic lupus erythematosus

Usually known as lupus, or SLE, this disease is a systemic autoimmune disorder producing a chronic inflammatory disease affecting all the organs of the body. Between 3 and 4 people in 100,000 suffer with this rheumatic disease and it is more commonly seen in Afro-Caribbeans and some Asian populations.

Lupus can be described as a type of self-allergy, in which the immune system, instead of protecting the body, turns and attacks the body's healthy tissues. This causes problems in all the systems of the body with sufferers experiencing some combination of fever, malaise, weight loss, skin eruptions, joint pain, breathing problems, kidney damage and gastrointestinal disorders. The typical rash on the face is a significant symptom and, because the marks were once believed to resemble wolf bites, has become part of the name of the disease (lupus).

Lupus is nine times more common in women than in men. Some 80-90% of sufferers now live for more than 10 years following diagnosis. Many of the drugs used to treat lupus suppress the function of the immune system, thus exposing the patient to an increasing risk of infection. Lupus can be caused by a virus, by exposure to sunlight, by infection or by certain drugs.

Psoriatic arthritis

Arthritis can be associated with psoriasis. Psoriatic arthritis is a form of inflammation of the joints in people who already have psoriasis or who may develop psoriasis in the future. Psoriasis is a scaly, flaking skin and nail disease, which can be quite severe. Psoriasis affects about 1 in 50 of the population and about 1 in 10 of those with psoriasis will develop the associated arthritis. It is not possible to predict which psoriasis sufferers will go on to develop joint problems. Psoriatic arthritis can affect all ages and both women and men are affected in equal numbers.

Infectious arthritis

Arthritis may occur as a consequence of direct infection of the joints by micro-organisms, or, less commonly, as a reaction to a preceding infection. This form of arthritis is usually curable provided that it is treated promptly and properly. Without treatment, however, infectious arthritis can lead to serious damage to the joints and it may spread to other parts of the body. There are three major kinds of germs that can cause infections and these are bacteria, viruses and fungi.

Septic arthritis

This is a serious and frequently fatal complication and is seen particularly in people with severe and debilitating nodular disease who are receiving steroids for arthritis. There may be an earlier history of an infected lesion such as an ingrowing toenail, boil or an ulcerating nodule. Septic arthritis causes the joint to be very hot and painful and the joint to be disproportionally inflamed compared with the arthritis in the other joints of the body. Immediate medical treatment should be sought.

HIV-associated rheumatic disease syndromes

HIV-associated rheumatic disease syndromes are a group of inflammatory musculoskeletal complications seen during the course of HIV infection. Painful joints are usually the first and most common rheumatic manifestation of the disorder but pain in the joints can occur at any stage of HIV infection. Other distinct rheumatic disorders, such as Reiter's syndrome, psoriatic arthritis, polymyositis, Sjögren's-like syndrome, lupus-like syndrome, vasculitis and fibromyalgia can also occur.

Sjögren's syndrome

In this disorder chronic arthritis is accompanied by dry eyes and dry mouth. Other symptoms include irritation, a gritty feeling or painful burning in the eyes. The eyelids may stick together. Food is difficult to chew and swallow because it sticks in the throat. The voice may be thin and reedy and the teeth may start to degenerate. Treatment is usually the same as for RA.

Fibromyalgia

Some people with arthritis also suffer with fibromyalgia, sometimes called fibrositis. This is a very common condition that is associated with widespread aching, stiffness and fatigue. It originates in the muscles and soft tissues of the body. People with fibromyalgia are found to have multiple tender points in specific muscle areas. Most sufferers complain of aching and stiffness in the areas around the neck, shoulders, upper back, lower back and hips. There may also be pain in the chest, knees and buttocks. The disease does not usually cause restriction of movement.

Many people with fibromyalgia have no underlying disorders, while others who develop fibromyalgia may already have conditions such as RA or arthritis of the spine. Fibromyalgia sufferers often suffer with sleep disturbance, irritable bowel syndrome and bladder problems.

Polymyalgia rheumatica

PMR is a disorder typically suffered by people over the age of 50. The disorder causes severe stiffness and aching in the neck, shoulder and hip areas. Other symptoms of PMR, which help to distinguish it from arthritis, include fatigue, weight loss, low fever and depression.

PMR rarely strikes before the age of 50, and the average age of people with this disease is about 70. PMR occurs twice as often in women as in men.

Chapter 2

Arthritis: Causes and Risk Factors

Arthritis, in its many forms, has a number of varied and complex causes. In some forms of the disease, age is the primary cause, in others a breakdown in the body's highly sophisticated chemistry, or a malfunction of the immune system.

Research topics currently under way into the cause of arthritis include understanding how the body's immune system works and what goes wrong in many types of arthritis.

The following pages deal with the risk factors for arthritis. Some of these risk factors are within your own control – you can lose weight, you can stop smoking and you can make general improvements to your lifestyle.

AGE

Age is a cause of some types of arthritis and a determining factor in other types.

In OA, the most common type of arthritis, nearly 70 per cent of people over the age of 70 have some arthritis visible on X-ray and it is without doubt a 'wear and tear' disease, a normal part of the ageing process.

In rheumatoid arthritis, an inflammatory autoimmune disease rather than a degenerative disease, age may be a determining factor, but it is not a cause. The usual age of onset for RA is 25 to 50.

It is clear that the development of gout is related to age but it is not caused by age. Many years of indulging in rich, high-protein foods and alcohol may eventually lead to the formation of uric acid crystals, which are responsible for the characteristic pain of gout.

Age plays a determining role in the development of ankylosing spondylitis without being a cause of the disease. The usual age of onset is 17 to 27.

Systemic lupus erythematosus usually affects women between the ages of 15 and 45 (the child-bearing years), although it can, in significantly fewer numbers, affect younger and older women and men as well.

Most diseases become worse with increasing age – there are few diseases that we are fortunate enough to 'grow out of'. Therefore, while age may be not be a cause of the majority of the different types of arthritis, the ageing process naturally plays its part in the acceleration of the disease itself and the weakening of our body's immune and defence mechanisms, thus rendering the body less able to fight the disease.

TOO MUCH WEIGHT

People who are carrying too much body weight are, clearly, putting a strain on all the systems of the body. The joints of the musculoskeletal system are no exception: they suffer an increased workload if you are overweight. What is normally a degenerative or wear and tear disease in people of average weight becomes a risk to health in obese people.

The delicate mechanisms of joints are sorely stretched when confronted with a burden in excess of their capability. The vertebrae of the spine become compressed. The cartilage surrounding the ends of bone becomes less springy. Muscles and joints require more oxygen to do the work required of them – but the overweight body cannot produce sufficient oxygen quickly enough to meet the demand.

THE HEREDITY FACTOR

Many types of arthritis can be seen to occur with greater frequency in some families than in others. However, this is not to say that arthritis is 'inherited'. The most that one can say is that you may have a genetic predisposition to that disease if your parents, grandparents, uncles and aunts have it.

THE GENETIC FACTOR

More than one gene has been implicated in the development of arthritis, notably rheumatoid arthritis. However, just because you have that gene, it does not necessarily mean to say that you will inevitably go on to develop the disease. Equally, some people who do not carry that gene may develop the disease.

The cause of arthritis and the search for the responsible gene is still a matter of concentrated scientific research. Genetic factors are known to play a role in predisposing people to rheumatoid arthritis, for example, but scientists do not yet know about all the specific genes that are involved.

THE GENDER FACTOR

Ankylosing spondylitis is one of the few forms of arthritis which are more common in men than in women. Most other types, however, are more often seen in women than in men.

The United States offers the biggest, and therefore the statistically most significant samples, in order to enable us to answer this question:

- ☐ In the USA nearly 23 million women of all ages are affected by arthritis. This accounts for nearly two thirds of all Americans with the disease.
- ☐ OA affects 11.7 million women which represents 74 per cent of all cases.
- ☐ Fibromyalgia affects 3.7 million people and seven times more women than men.
- ☐ Rheumatoid arthritis affects 1.5 million women which represents 71 per cent of cases.
- ☐ SLE affects 117,000 women which represents 89 per cent of all cases.
- ☐ JRA affects 61,000 girls which represents 86 per cent of all cases.

EXERCISE AND SPORT

In the normal way, exercise is a thoroughly beneficial practice to incorporate into our lives, and most of us would gain by doing more exercise than we already do. This said, there are certain forms of exercise and sport which can aggravate arthritis if you are already predisposed to it and certain forms that may actually cause the disease.

Ballet dancers notoriously suffer with arthritis, sometimes when they are still dancing and, more often, after their dancing career has finished. The stresses and strains of ballet positions and techniques placed upon the joints of the body represent an intolerable burden and the joints suffer. It is usually osteoarthritis, the wear and tear disease, that dancers suffer from in later years.

Contact sports are notorious for causing joint problems, cartilage problems and arthritis in later years. Football is probably the best known example.

The main problems in exercise and sport are:

☐ The repetitive nature of some exercise. For example, jogging places considerable strain on the knees and the vertebrae of the spine. Cycling, if practised to an extreme, causes significant wear and tear on the knees.

☐ The increased potential for trauma (injury).

☐ That many forms of exercise and sport are competitive in nature and, therefore, the body is in a state of tension, which itself increases the potential for trauma and wear and tear. Racing and competitive skiing, for example, both require an unnatural position to be held for some time, while the body is in an acute tension state: again, the knees and the hips suffer.

If you do suffer aches and pains after sport or exercise, take this as a warning: your body is telling you that the strain is too much. Don't be tempted to ignore the warning. Take a few days out for rest and allow the body to recuperate.

MEDICATION

Because some drugs can interact with others and some combinations of drugs can produce unwanted side-effects in the form of arthritis, it is essential that you check with your doctor before taking any medication.

Your doctor should be aware of all the other drugs that you are taking so that they can check for drug interaction. This is especially important in gout, for example, because the very treatment that can relieve other types of arthritis, aspirin, can promote gout.

Arthritis drugs can interact with ACE inhibitors (prescribed for lowering blood pressure) and lithium (a psychotropic drug prescribed for mania and some types of depression). Rubella vaccination can produce short-lived arthritis, as does rubella itself. The vaccination produces musculoskeletal symptoms in 20 per cent of cases. These usually last for two to four weeks after the vaccination, but they may persist for several weeks, and, in rare cases, months. Intravenous drug users are at risk of developing septic arthritis.

When you receive a prescription from your doctor:

1. Check that it is made out for what the doctor was intending to prescribe.
2. Ask your doctor if there are known side-effects of the drug, so that you know what to expect.
3. When you have the drug made up at the pharmacy, check that what you have been given is what your doctor intended to prescribe.

Mistakes can and do happen: human error is part of everyday life.

ALLERGIES

Allergy can be defined as a damaging immune response of the body to a substance (especially a particular food, pollen, fur or dust) to which it has become hypersensitive.

A large number of allergies can produce symptoms of arthritis. It is important that you ask your doctor to refer you for hospital allergy investigations if you are suffering arthritis pains without any other evidence of arthritis and you suspect an allergy.

TRAUMA (INJURY)

Arthritis sometimes develops after an injury that damages a joint whether or not you have a genetic predisposition to the disease. The arthritis may develop many years after the trauma. This type of arthritis is known as secondary arthritis.

Part II: Helping Yourself To Alleviate Your Arthritis – Your Lifestyle

Chapter 3

Your Diet

A healthy, balanced diet is a must for all of us whether or not we suffer with arthritis. The term 'balanced' simply means a diet that adequately meets your nutritional needs while not providing any nutrients in excess. A balanced diet provides optimal protein and complex carbohydrates while containing only moderate amounts of salt, fats and simple sugars.

While carbohydrates, fats and protein are the essential elements of a healthy diet, it is simpler to look at the different foods that we eat in four groups, grouped by the similarity of their nutrients.

In order to achieve a balanced diet, you need to consume a variety of foods, every day, from each of the **four food groups** shown below. However, arthritis sufferers need to take into account the fact that diet plays a part in the illness. You will find, therefore, in the remainder of this chapter, all the information you need concerning suspect foods which may aggravate arthritis, as well as information concerning the vitamin and mineral supplements that you may wish to add to your normal diet.

1. Protein, in the form of meat, poultry and fish.
2. Smaller amounts of protein and calcium from dairy products such as eggs, cheese, milk and milk products.

3. Protein from nuts, peas, beans, lentils, soya and pulses. (Peas and beans, as well as other vegetables, also provide us with essential vitamins.)
4. Carbohydrates and fibre from pulses and grains (and to a much lesser extent from fruit and vegetables) in the form of barley and bran, for example.

You should eat from these four groups every day, and also drink at least 8 glasses of water a day (and preferably more).

DO YOU NEED TO LOSE WEIGHT?

One of the measures used to assess healthy weight is the Body Mass Index (BMI). This is considered to be a healthier measure than weight tables.

To calculate your BMI:
1. Convert your weight to kilograms by dividing your weight in pounds (undressed) by 2.2.
2. Convert your height in inches to metres by dividing it by 39.4, then square it.
3. Divide the result of 1 by the result of 2. This is your Body Mass Index.

For example, if your weight is 65 kg, and height 1.68 metres, first multiply 1.68 by 1.68 = 2.82. Next, divide 65 by your answer (2.82). Your BMI is 23.

Most health experts and nutritionists agree that a BMI of over 40 is a serious health risk, but those of us with a BMI of 25 to 30 need not be too concerned.

People with a BMI of between 20 and 25 – the optimum measure – have a lower risk of illnesses such as heart disease, high blood pressure and stroke.

Those with a BMI of 25 to 30 have a moderate risk and those with a BMI of over 30 a proportionately greater risk. The over 30 group is also more likely to contract diseases, such as arthritis, affecting the joints and muscles.

RELIEVING ARTHRITIS SYMPTOMS THROUGH YOUR DIET

Doctors are now taking diet seriously because in recent years there has been an increasing amount of evidence that nutrition plays an important part in arthritis, particularly in rheumatoid arthritis. Research shows that changing what you eat can help relieve symptoms. You may not be able to cure rheumatoid arthritis with diet, but it can mean less pain, shorter periods of stiffness, and a stronger grip. Some people who change their diet are able to reduce – or even give up – drugs. Others are helped by a combination of dietary changes and medication. There are some people, however, who do not seem to benefit much by changing their diet.

TREATING RHEUMATOID ARTHRITIS WITH DIET

The basics are:
- ☐ Find out what foods you are sensitive to.
- ☐ Eliminate them from your diet.
- ☐ Take certain supplements.
- ☐ Eat healthy, nutritious food.

Food sensitivity

Food sensitivities and dietary fat can help cause rheumatoid arthritis. Although people with rheumatoid arthritis do not display classic allergy reactions to particular foods, many develop symptoms when they eat them and stop getting symptoms when they do not. This means they are sensitive to certain foods. When you are sensitive to particular foods, the body's immune response is altered. Food sensitivities can develop when you eat the same foods day in, day out, so be careful not to eat the same every day.

Foods to avoid

- ☐ **Beef, pork** and other **red meat.**
- ☐ **Wheat and other grains** such as barley, oats and rye.
- ☐ **Sugar** and sweet things.

☐ **Fat and fried food.** Some fats can have an inflammatory effect.

☐ **Salt.** Salt is added to snacks, processed meals, tinned soups and sauces.

☐ **Caffeine.** This is found in coffee, tea, cola and chocolate.

☐ **Dairy produce.** This includes milk, cheese, cream, milk products, dairy ice-cream.

☐ **Pulses.** Pulses such as lentils contain a substance called lectin, which can aggravate arthritis symptoms.

☐ **Tomatoes, white potatoes, all peppers, aubergines (also tobacco).** These belong to the nightshade group of plants and contain solanine, which if not destroyed in the intestines can be toxic.

☐ **Smoked and processed meats.** These include bacon, sausages, luncheon meats.

☐ **Alcohol.** Certain alcoholic drinks give more problems than others. Heavy drinking can also weaken the bones.

☐ **Fizzy drinks.** The phosphates in fizzy drinks deplete calcium levels.

☐ **Refined carbohydrates.** These include white bread, white flour and all products made with it.

☐ **Additives and preservatives.**

☐ **Acidic foods** such as vinegar, orange juice and citrus fruits.

☐ **Chocolate.**

☐ **Eggs, nuts and seeds, onions.**

Which foods are suspect?

Certain foods do aggravate arthritis, but there are individual differences. One way to find out which foods aggravate your arthritis is to keep a diary of what you eat and note whether you experience pain, discomfort, swelling or stiffness afterwards. Practitioners use other methods to test for food sensitivities, including blood tests and applied kinesiology.

Going on an elimination diet

Once you have identified the foods that you think may be causing symptoms, you should cut them from your diet for a month and subsequently reintroduce them one by one to see whether or not your symptoms return. It is the only accurate and reliable way to confirm reactions to foods. An elimination diet should, ideally, be undertaken with medical supervision.

Why are you sensitive to certain foods?

Problems in the gut

Rheumatoid arthritis may develop because of long-term bacterial infection in the gut. Infection and inflammation can happen when the contents of the intestines, including foods, bacteria, or their breakdown products, are absorbed through the damaged lining of gut walls. Food sensitivities are caused by problems in the gut. Changes in the diet can alter the bacterial activity in the gut and bring about an improvement.

Candida albicans

This is a fungal proliferation in the gut. It can be a cause or contributing factor in arthritis. It is made worse by eating yeast and sugary foods, but it can be treated with anti-fungal foods and drugs.

What is the best diet for rheumatoid arthritis?

Many people with rheumatoid arthritis are not eating a healthy diet. According to the journal, *Arthritis and Rheumatism,* only six per cent of sufferers consume the recommended daily intake of selenium, which helps protect against arthritis, and only 23 per cent eat enough calcium, which is essential for strong bones. So, ensure that you are eating a healthy, balanced and nutritious diet.

You can eat plenty of:

☐ **Fish and seafood.** All fish are good (except for gout sufferers), especially cold water oily fish like mackerel, sardines, herring, salmon, halibut, trout, tuna. Eat at least five fish meals a week. (*See also Gout.*)

☐ **Chicken, turkey (with the skin removed), veal**. Eat these instead of red meat.

☐ **Vegetables**. Go for green, leafy, raw and fresh. Dark green vegetables contain the essential fatty acid, alpha-linolenic acid. Have a salad a day. Steam or microwave vegetables to keep in all the nutrients. Try and eat at least one totally vegetarian meal a week.

☐ **Fruits**. All fruits are fine. They also replace the sweetness when you give up white sugar. Fruit and vegetables are a good source of fibre.

☐ **Polyunsaturated oils**. Found in seed oils like sunflower, safflower. Add linseeds, sunflower seeds and unrefined oils to your diet.

☐ **Wholefoods**. Wholegrain bread and brown rice are high in fibre. Complex carbohydrates are digested more slowly than refined carbohydrates.

☐ **Water**. Water is needed for many vital body functions. Filtered or bottled spring water is better than tap water.

The naturopathic diet

For rheumatoid arthritis, naturopaths recommend a diet high in wholegrains, vegetables and fibre, and low in sugar, animal-derived foods and refined carbohydrates.

Fasting and partial fasting

Fasting reduces disease activity in rheumatoid arthritis and is sometimes used to good effect during flare-ups. Fasting is supposed to promote health because it gives all the organs of the body a complete rest, toxins are eliminated, the system cleansed, and the liver activated. Arthritis almost always improves when people stop eating, which shows that food may play a part in aggravating arthritis. Fasting changes the blood chemistry, slowing down the action of certain enzymes and blocking key steps in the chain of events that lead to inflammation and pain. In naturopathic and Ayurvedic medicine, fasting is common.

In a partial fast, you can have things like herbal teas, vegetable juice extracts and fruit juices. People are sometimes put on a partial fast for around 7 to 10 days to clean out the system before starting an elimination diet.

Supplements for rheumatoid arthritis

Taking supplements can make up for any deficiency in the diet. Some supplements have particular anti-inflammatory effects. Many of the following supplements have been tested in scientific trials.

- ☐ **Fish oils.** Fish oils contain important fatty acids, called EPA and DHA, which are anti-inflammatory. Research shows that taking a high dose of fish oils – 3 grams a day – produces a modest improvement in joint pain and stiffness. Fish oil alone, without making any changes to the diet, can bring about improvements. You need to take a daily dose of fish oil for at least three to six months for it to be effective.

- ☐ **Gammalinolenic acid – found in evening primrose oil, borage seed (starflower) oil, blackcurrant seed oil.** GLA is another kind of essential fatty acid. It converts to a prostaglandin called E1, known to have an anti-inflammatory effect. Taking 6 grams a day can help reduce morning stiffness and other symptoms. When fish oils and GLA are taken together, it may sometimes be possible to reduce or even stop treatment with anti-inflammatory drugs.

- ☐ **Antioxidants.** Antioxidants are nutrients which scavenge dangerous free radicals in the body and are anti-inflammatory. Antioxidants include **vitamin E.** Rheumatoid arthritis causes inflamed joints, which in turn depletes the joints of vitamin E. A daily intake of 600iu a day has been shown to help rheumatoid arthritis. Other antioxidants include **Pycnogenol.** These are botanicals containing antioxidants, especially extract of the bark of maritime pine and grape seed extract.

- ☐ **Vitamin B5.** In rheumatoid arthritis, there may be a deficiency of B5 (also known as pantothenic acid). It aids tissue repair. Some nutritionally oriented doctors suggest 1,000mg of vitamin B5 to help with morning stiffness, general disability and pain.

- □ **Vitamin B6**. Helps reduce swelling and joint stiffness.
- □ **Vitamin C**. Useful if you are taking aspirin, as aspirin depletes the body of vitamin C. Vitamin C can be low in rheumatoid arthritis, possibly because of free radical activity in inflamed areas. Vitamin C is a free radical scavenger and also necessary for cartilage and bone formation.
- □ **Zinc**. Zinc metabolism is altered in rheumatoid arthritis and patients are often low in zinc. Working with other nutrients, zinc also has a role to play in reducing inflammation.
- □ **New Zealand green lipid mussel**. This is an extract of the New Zealand green lipped mussel. It may have a mild anti-inflammatory effect.
- □ **Selenium**. There is a relationship between low levels of the trace element selenium and rheumatoid arthritis. People with the condition seem to have an abnormality in the metabolism of selenium.
- □ **Other supplements**. Kelp, royal jelly, ginseng, cider vinegar, garlic and honey are thought to help arthritis sufferers.

Herbs

- □ Boswellia, used in the Ayurvedic system of medicine, has anti-inflammatory action, similar to non-steroidal anti-inflammatory drugs but without the side-effects.
- □ Turmeric. This is the yellow spice used in curry dishes. It is anti-inflammatory, and protects against free radicals.
- □ Ginger is also anti-inflammatory.
- □ Yucca tea, 7 or 8 grams of the root boiled in a pint of water for 15 minutes, is often drunk for symptom relief. It can be taken three to five times a day.
- □ Burdock root, Devil's claw, horsetail, sarsaparilla and white willow can also be useful.

OSTEOARTHRITIS AND DIET

The best way to prevent osteoarthritis is believed to be to have a good intake of foods containing **calcium** from an early age to build healthy bones. Calcium is found in milk, cheese, sardines and pilchards (especially with bones), broccoli, milk chocolate, digestive biscuits, spinach, cereals and muesli, and figs. Foods that inhibit calcium absorption, such as fizzy drinks, should be avoided.

Adequate amounts of **vitamin D**, needed for calcium absorption, are also needed to prevent osteoporosis. Obesity increases the risk of osteoarthritis, so a low-fat, low-calorie diet may be able to help.

Dietary supplements for osteoarthritis

Calcium. Calcium supplements have to be strong enough to do any good. Take calcium citrate or chelated calcium.

Glucosamine sulphate. This is derived from sea shells which contains a building-block needed for the repair of joint cartilage. Symptoms may be lessened and damaged joints repaired if you take 500mg 3 times a day.

Chondroitin sulphate. Levels of chondroitin sulphate may be reduced in joint cartilage affected by osteoarthritis and possibly other forms of arthritis. It may help restore joint function. Glucosamine sulphate and chondroitin sulphate can be taken in combination.

Vitamin B6. This is needed to help the absorption of glucosamine sulphate and chondroitin sulphate.

Antioxidants. Those who eat high levels of antioxidants show a much slower rate of joint deterioration, particularly in the knees. **Vitamin E,** 400-600iu a day, has been shown to reduce the symptoms of osteoarthritis. **Pycnogenols** have a similar effect.

Vitamin C with bioflavonoids. Vitamin C is an antioxidant, but it also strengthens collagen, the cell-binding protein found in bone. Collagen cannot be synthesised without vitamin C. Recommended intake is 3+ grams a day. Vitamin E can be taken with vitamin C. The two nutrients together help reduce inflammation and speed up the healing of joints.

Boron. Boron affects calcium metabolism, and a link between boron deficiency and arthritis has been suggested. 6mg of boron per day, taken for two months, may help relieve symptoms of osteoarthritis.

However, as boron can increase oestrogen levels, boron supplements should be limited to 1mg per day. Sources include bee pollen and kelp.

Magnesium. Needed for the maintenance of healthy bones.

Fish oils (see above). Fish oils may also play a role in osteoarthritis.

Vitamin D. Essential for good bone formation, growth and maintenance. You get it from exposure to sunshine and eating oily fish or cod liver oil.

Zinc. Needed for cross-linking and regeneration of connective tissue in cartilage.

Niacinamide (also called nicotinamide). A form of vitamin B3. High doses (250mg 4-16 times a day) can help increase joint mobility, improve muscle strength and decrease fatigue.

D-phenylalanine. This amino acid has been used to treat chronic pain – including osteoarthritis – with variable effectiveness.

B Vitamins. B12, folic acid and vitamin K may help bone formation.

Herbs

- Herbs rich in calcium include parsley, dandelion leaf, horsetail and nettle.
- Boswellia has unique anti-inflammatory action, working in a similar way to non-steroidal anti-inflammatory drugs.
- Horsetail is believed to have the effect of strengthening connective tissue. It is rich in silica, which helps harden bones.
- White willow has anti-inflammatory and pain-relieving effects.
- Chinese angelica, liquorice, false unicorn root, black cohosh, wild yam and sage are plants that contain compounds similar to oestrogen, but are less powerful than synthetic hormones and produce fewer side-effects.

Above all, remember that balance is the keyword in diet: eat from as wide a range of foods as possible every day while eliminating those that you suspect make your condition worse.

Chapter 4

Exercise and Specific Exercises

Exercise is one of the most important things you can do to alleviate the discomfort of arthritis and to some extent to lessen the likelihood of the joints becoming stiff and arthritic.

Exercise protects against loss of joint function, keeps joints and muscles working, and helps prevent disability. It reduces joint pain and stiffness and increases flexibility, muscle strength and endurance. Exercise also helps you lose weight and contributes to a greater sense of well-being through the release of endorphins. If you do not exercise, you lose muscle strength and joints can become unstable and painful. Being inactive usually increases arthritis problems.

How much and what exercise you do very much depends on what type of arthritis you have and how badly it affects you. Even if many of your joints are affected, you still need to exercise. Be cautious, however, about exercising when you are having a flare-up – only do gentle Range-Of-Movement Exercises. If possible, have an exercise programme tailor-made to your needs by a physiotherapist. Make exercise a part of your daily routine. It is best to exercise when you have least pain, least stiffness, and your medication is having the most effect.

WHAT TYPES OF EXERCISE ARE BEST FOR ARTHRITIS?

There are three different types of exercise:
- ☐ Stretching or Range-Of-Motion (ROM).
- ☐ Strengthening and muscle conditioning.
- ☐ Aerobic or endurance.

They each have a different function, and one type of exercise is not a substitute for another.

☐ **Stretching or range-of-motion** exercises gently move your joints through their full range of movement as far as they can go. This type of exercise helps maintain normal joint movement, relieves stiffness and increases flexibility. Stretching exercises should be done twice a day, with periods of rest. Some people find it gets them going first thing in the morning. Ideally, they should be performed three to ten times a session, depending on your pain level. By doing this, many people see an improvement in their range of movements.

☐ **Strengthening and muscle conditioning** exercises are useful when you have lost strength in particular joints. They contract the muscle around the joint without actually moving the joint itself, thus increasing muscle strength. Start with muscle-strengthening exercises once a day, contracting a muscle for one or two seconds. As you get stronger, gradually build this up so that you are holding for a count of six seconds, then relax and repeat four times, twice a day.

☐ **Aerobic or endurance** exercises improve your overall function, promote cardiovascular fitness, increase bone strength and reduce fatigue. They help reduce inflammation in the joints and keep your weight down. Aerobic exercises are more active, such as walking, running, swimming, aerobic dancing, aquatics, or cycling. Aim to do this kind of exercise for 20 minutes two to three times a week.

GETTING THE MOST OUT OF EXERCISE

☐ Don't expect miracles immediately. If you have already lost some function in your joints, it can take a while to regain it.

☐ Always begin by stretching and warming up.

☐ Start with easy, range-of-motion exercises.

☐ Add low-impact aerobics when you feel ready.

☐ Start strengthening exercises slowly with small weights.

☐ If you enjoy your exercises, you're more likely to stick with them.

☐ Rest when you need to. Get the balance right between exercise and rest.

☐ Expect some normal exercise discomfort. But, if you feel any pain, STOP.

HOW MUCH EXERCISE SHOULD YOU DO?

It depends on how fit you are and how bad your arthritis is. Ideally, you should do some kind of endurance exercise twice a week and stretching (range-of-movement) exercises every day. You may feel tired, but a little endurance exercise like a short walk is likely to make you feel less fatigued.

However, you can exercise too much. If you have more pain two hours after exercising than you did before, do less next time. Warning signs that you are doing too much include unusual or persistent fatigue, swollen joints, or decreased range of motion. If your joints become painful, inflamed or red, STOP.

EXERCISES SUITABLE FOR ARTHRITIS

Walking

Walking is an ideal exercise for people with arthritis. It is weight-bearing, easy on the joints, and uses most of the body's major muscles. It can also help you lose weight.

If you do hill walking, you can help build up the muscles in your legs and thighs. Walkers with strengthened muscles have greater joint stability and less pain. There is evidence that taking part in a supervised walking programme can alleviate the pain associated with osteoarthritis of the knees.

Spend around 10 to 15 minutes doing warm-up exercises – gently stretching the muscles of your arms and legs. Start walking at an easy pace for about five minutes, increasing your speed gradually to a brisk pace of about 3 to 4 mph. Try and maintain this pace for around 15 to 20 minutes. For the final 5 minutes, slow down again. At the end, stretch for another 5 to 10 minutes to help keep your muscles loose. If you forget to stretch and begin to feel pain, you could be put off.

If you haven't done much exercise before, start out slowly and gradually build up your distance. Start with a 15 to 30 minute walk, three times a week. As you get fitter, you could walk for longer, adding hills to the route. Don't push yourself if it hurts.

It does not take long to see improvements. If you walk regularly, you should notice a difference in just a month. You may find that you weigh less, have more energy and sleep better. Even if you do not weigh less, you may look slimmer as your muscles tighten up. You will also have the satisfaction of knowing you are doing something to alleviate arthritic pain. If you make walking a regular habit, you are more likely to stick to it.

Exercising in water

Water takes the weight off your body so that you can do more with less pain.

Swimming is excellent as it exercises your whole body and the water carries your weight. If your local hospital has a warm **hydrotherapy** pool, ask your doctor to refer you. Many council swimming pools offer **aquarobic classes** with qualified teachers. If you can find someone else with arthritis to go with, it may be more fun. Be careful not to overdo it in the water.

Golf

If you have arthritis in your hands you could build up the grips of your clubs with foam pads to reduce the pressure on the joints. Instead of carrying your bag, you could rent a cart. Make sure that you do plenty of warm-up exercises, which should include stretching your back, hips and shoulders, and range-of-motion exercises for your elbows, wrists and hands. Taking a hot bath or shower before playing can also help you feel more flexible.

Other forms of exercise that you may like to try include bowling, dance therapy, T'ai Chi and yoga.

EXERCISE PROGRAMME FOR PEOPLE WITH ARTHRITIS

Keeping your neck supple

You can stretch your neck muscles and loosen up any tightness by following these exercises:

1. Sit straight on an upright chair, bend your neck slowly to one side, trying to touch your shoulder with your ear.
2. Straighten your neck and now repeat on the other side.
3. Repeat these sequences five to ten times.
4. Sitting on the upright chair, slowly rotate your neck to one side as if you were trying to look behind you.
5. Straighten your neck and repeat on the other side.
6. Repeat this sequence five times.

You can keep the back and shoulder muscles flexible by performing these exercises

1. Sit on an upright chair with your arms hanging down on either side of the chair. Swivel the top half of your body round to the left-hand side, moving your left arm over the back of the chair and placing your left hand over your right thigh.
2. Repeat this five to ten times on each side.

The following exercises help hip flexibility

1. Stand behind an upright chair, holding the back as a support, swing out the left leg as far as you can, provided that you feel no pain.
2. Keep the other leg straight and hold your body upright. Do not allow your body to lean away from the leg you are swinging out.
3. Repeat these two movements five to ten times on each side of the body.

Exercises for the hands

You can do these anywhere at any time, such as when you are watching television or waiting in a queue:

EXERCISE AND SPECIFIC EXERCISES

1. Spread out your hands in front of you. Bend each finger in turn and then relax each finger before you move the next.
2. Rotate your wrists to increase the circulation to the fingers, first in one direction and then in the opposite direction.
3. Repeat these two exercises five to ten times at least once a day.

Chapter 5

Reducing Stress

We all need some stress and pressure in our lives in order to keep the adrenaline flowing and to enjoy the buzz of having something to do. However, each of us has an individual stress level beyond which we cannot function, in either body or mind, as efficiently as we would normally.

It is so common for us to feel tired all the time that family doctors abbreviate it in their patients' medical notes as TATT. But it doesn't have to be like that. You can regain your energy and start living life to the full once again. First of all, assess your life.

Look at the three principal different elements of your life:

☐ Your work life (paid and unpaid).

☐ Your friends and family life.

☐ Your personal life.

DO YOU HAVE A GOOD BALANCE IN YOUR LIFE?

Are you able to spend time with close friends and family?

Do you get time to do those things that refresh you and recharge your batteries – things that do not fall into the task category or relationship category?

Balance in your life is essential if you are to reach your potential and to enjoy life without feeling constantly stressed out.

Be generous to yourself: give yourself time to read, to get out in the fresh air, to go to a film, to do whatever it is that you personally can become absorbed in.

Once you have made time for yourself, you will have the energy to meet the challenges made by the other areas of your life.

TRY ANY OF THESE RAPID DE-STRESSORS:

- ☐ A regular dance class at your local adult education institute (evening class).
- ☐ Laugh with a comic novel.
- ☐ A long walk by the seashore.
- ☐ Have a vigorous game of tennis (or squash if it is raining).
- ☐ Help someone that you know is in need – what you give out is what you get back – they may need company or help with some home or garden task.
- ☐ Paint and draw.
- ☐ Plan a wonderful surprise for a close friend or your partner.
- ☐ Sessions in a flotation tank.
- ☐ Consultations with osteopath or chiropractor.

DON'TS:

- ☐ Avoid stretching yourself too thin or you and everyone around you will suffer.
- ☐ Never try and buck yourself up with coffee, chocolate or crisps: in the long run they will make your body ache more than it did before.
- ☐ Don't feel that you have to take on everything that you are asked to do – learn how to say No for the sake of your physical and emotional health.

DO YOU NEED TO:

- ☐ Sort out long-term problems?
- ☐ Banish the negative forces from your life?
- ☐ Resolve dilemmas?
- ☐ Dejunk your life and home of all the clutter?
- ☐ Take the window boxes/plants/garden in hand?

AND, TO DO THAT, YOU MAY NEED TO:

- ☐ Reassess your belief in yourself and raise your self-esteem.
- ☐ Deal with ongoing stresses in your life.

☐ Examine your core beliefs and make changes to your lifestyle.

☐ Take a clean broom to your life with renewed positive energy.

☐ You CAN do anything you want to do.

STRESSING THE BODY

Too much stress is toxic to both body and mind. When we are stressed, certain brain chemicals are activated, setting off a very complex set of chain reactions in the body. Pain in the joints and muscles often becomes more pronounced during times of stress, when we are feeling tired and when tension builds up in the body. The end result of these stress reactions can cause disorders such as:

☐ Headache.

☐ Backache.

☐ Aches and pains.

☐ Stiffness caused by tension in the joints and muscles.

☐ Unexplained anger.

☐ Depression.

☐ Anxiety.

☐ Apathy.

☐ Chronic fatigue.

☐ Migraine.

☐ Eczema.

☐ Asthma.

☐ Sneezing fits.

☐ Raised blood pressure.

☐ Heart attack.

☐ Stroke.

There are many different causes of stress, from the necessity of staying in a disliked job, an unsatisfactory home or family relationship, divorce, bereavement, lack of money, or ill health to, simply, too much to do in not enough time.

The key to alleviating stress is three-fold:

☐ Prioritise.

☐ Eliminate.

☐ Delegate.

WHAT MATTERS MOST: YOUR PRIORITIES

Sit down and write out all the things that you have to do in their order of importance to You.

Of these priorities, can you simply eliminate some or put them on a back burner?

Which of your priorities can you delegate to others? You don't have to do everything yourself.

Only by having a careful look a your priorities in this way can you reduce your workload and in this way start to overcome stress.

DON'T SWEAT IT: ELIMINATE THE SMALL STUFF

Not everything that we do in our lives – whether it be our work life, our family and relationship life or our personal life – necessarily has to be done. Really scrutinise your list to see what can be completely eliminated, thus freeing up some of your time.

SPARE YOURSELF: DELEGATE

Friends, family and paid help can all help to reduce your workload. Never be afraid to ask for help, especially at times of stress. People really like to be asked and to feel needed.

Once you have unlocked the causes of the stress in your life, you can start to take control by:

☐ Resolving dilemmas.

☐ Cutting out the dead wood.

☐ Setting goals.

One of the greatest causes of stress is unresolved problems and dilemmas which may drag on for years and years. For example, money worries, an unsatisfactory relationship or marriage, a friendship that causes only irritation rather than joy, a hobby that was once a pleasure which has turned into a chore, a job that you dislike.

Are there aspects of your life which invariably stress you? Which steps can you take to eliminate them or resolve them? Now is the time to set boundaries, to tell yourself that you do not have to put up with this situation/behaviour/whatever. You deserve better. By *knowing* that you deserve better, you will be able to achieve improvements in all areas of your life.

You cannot of course achieve everything at once: in some situations you may have to set intermediate goals (I will do this by that date and this by that date, for example) and monitor your progress. The important thing is to take the first step to resolving any situation that is stressing you. Once you have taken the first step, the second will be easier.

YOU YOURSELF HOLD ALL THE CARDS: ALL YOU HAVE TO DO IS PLAY THEM.

By taking control of your life in this way, you are already part of the way to overcoming stress and allowing your body to function fully, freely and flexibly in all its planes. Enjoy feeling the stress run out of your muscles and joints as you rethink the elements of your home life, your relationship life and your working life.

Chapter 6

The Importance of Sleep

The common symptoms of arthritis are alleviated to some extent by a good night's sleep. Our body is renewed and reinvigorated by sleep during the night. During the day, little by little, we are being worn out. It is during the night that all the billions of cells of the body are most quickly renewed. This renewal does take place during the day, too, but not so rapidly.

Our brain and nervous system is rested and refreshed during sleep because we are unable to react to what is going on around us. As well as the recuperation and renewal of cells, and the rest afforded the joints and muscles, most other processes of the body slow down so that we use less oxygen, our temperature falls and the heart rate slows.

As we sleep, the body's own natural cleansing system (the liver, the kidneys, the circulation) carry on with their work unimpeded by further onslaughts of toxins to process. This system may be of particular importance to arthritis sufferers.

Without enough sleep, we wake up feeling tired, sluggish and bleary. All our aches and pains are ever more acute. The metabolism is slow so that when we do eat to try to buck ourselves up, we do not burn the calories and store essential nutrients as well as we would if we were well-rested.

Because we are not ready to wake up, the eyes feel dry (the production of tear liquid decreases during sleep), our skin is dry and itchy, the joints ache, the legs ache, and we may feel cold, shivery, apathetic and unable to concentrate.

Sleep is an essential feature of any health programme and an essential feature of life for arthritis sufferers. Without good-quality, regular sleep, the body cannot benefit very greatly.

WHAT IS A GOOD SLEEP?

Good-quality sleep depends on these factors:

☐ Going to bed and getting up at roughly the same time respectively each night and each morning.

☐ Taking no food or stimulants such as tea, coffee, alcohol or nicotine for three hours before bedtime.

☐ Sleeping in a well-ventilated room (with a window open a little).

☐ Sleeping in a room free of distractions such as computer, TV, newspapers or work papers.

☐ Sleeping on a bed that gives you good support without being too hard.

☐ Sleeping in a quiet environment (earplugs if not).

☐ Putting off stimulating discussion (or a row) with partner or family until the next day.

☐ Not giving into temptation to get up and make a cup of tea if you cannot sleep.

IF YOU CANNOT SLEEP

Just lie there calmly and visualise the cells of the body renewing themselves. When you rest in a dark room, the body, although not the brain, is still capable of some regeneration.

Chapter 7

Detoxing and the Importance of Water

There is considerable controversy over the question of whether or not it is necessary to detox the body through certain diets, through fasting and through drinking large amounts of water.

Some health experts maintain that the body has all it needs in the way of liver, kidneys and the circulation to detox itself. Others maintain that because of the modern world's pollutants and toxins we need to detox our bodies regularly.

Advocates of detoxing claim that we can improve our health, raise our energy levels, fight off chronic fatigue and alleviate common disorders such as arthritis, headache, backache, mouth ulcers, irritable bowel syndrome, eczema, allergy and asthma.

Detoxing is said to tone up all the systems of your body, including the digestive system, the respiratory system, the cardiovascular system, the brain and the nervous system and all the joints and muscles of the body.

We are surrounded everywhere every day by toxins and pollutants in many different forms. It is not always practical to avoid some of these, but the least we can do for ourselves and for the health of our children is to avoid those toxins that we can, such as tobacco smoke and tar, alcohol and caffeine, and improve our own immune system.

EVERYTHING IN MODERATION: ONE-DAY DETOX PROGRAMME

Detoxing for several consecutive days is not recommended for arthritis sufferers. However, many people feel quite good after a

49

one-day detox programme. Here's what you do:

- ☐ When you wake up: a glass of water with a slice of lemon.
- ☐ One slice of wholemeal bread (no butter) to wake up the digestive system.
- ☐ 30 minutes' brisk exercise such as walking or running to start up your circulatory system, which assists in lymph drainage.
- ☐ A glass of liquidised fruit or vegetables for guaranteed detox.
- ☐ Dry skin brushing before bath or shower to remove dead cells and exfoliation cream for face, hands, feet and elbows.
- ☐ Two glasses of water to aid detox.
- ☐ Bath or shower with aromatherapy essential oils *(see Part III)*, wash hair and massage whole body afterwards.
- ☐ A game of tennis or squash, or whatever other exercise appeals to you.
- ☐ A glass of water.
- ☐ A salt rub after the exercise to help slough off dead skin and speed up the detox process.

(If you prefer, forget sports and turn out all the kitchen cupboards.)

- ☐ Late morning: a glass of water.
- ☐ At lunch time: a glass of water.
- ☐ Anything you like from salads, fruit, vegetables, pulses (beans and lentils), wholemeal bread (no butter and no salad dressings).
- ☐ Mid-afternoon: two glasses of water with a slice of lemon.
- ☐ One hour spent in some form of relaxation or relaxing exercise such as meditation, yoga, self-hypnosis, T'ai Chi, for example (don't succumb to mid-afternoon munchies or fall asleep!). Stick of celery or an apple if you like.
- ☐ Spend an hour assessing your lifestyle *(see the remaining chapters in Part II and Chapter 25)* and make a list of changes you wish to achieve.
- ☐ Make a cleansing soup such as carrot and tomato soup, white bean and lemon, broccoli or whatever vegetable and pulses appeal.
- ☐ Eat with wholemeal bread.
- ☐ Early evening: a glass of water.

- ☐ 20 minutes' skipping.
- ☐ 20 minutes' stretch and tone exercises.
- ☐ Mid-evening: a glass of water.
- ☐ Thoroughly cleanse and moisturise your face and apply exfoliating cream once again to your hands.
- ☐ Check that your bedroom conforms with the tips for good-quality sleep *(see Chapter 6)*.
- ☐ Go to bed at least an hour earlier than usual and before bed: a glass of water.

THE VALUE OF WATER

Some health experts favour detox programmes while others maintain they are unnecessary. However, all are agreed upon the necessity of drinking substantial amounts of water for optimum health.

All of us should drink at least eight glasses every day and preferably more. Some authorities maintain that two litres of water a day is necessary for optimum health.

If you use this 64 oz standard as a base, it is suggested that you drink an additional 8 oz (approximately 250 ml) for every 25 pounds (approximately 11.5 kg) over your ideal weight.

Most medical authorities now suggest a basic standard of 1 oz of water for every two pounds of body weight.

Whichever method you chose, you should increase your normal intake during hot weather and when engaging in exercise or any physically strenuous activity. Keep some bottled water with you all the time and sip frequently.

Chapter 8

Smoking, Drinking and Other Drugs

Few smokers can claim ignorance of the medical hazards of smoking. Cigarette smoking causes over 100,000 premature deaths a year in Great Britain, 23,000 premature deaths in Australia every year and some 350,000 annually in the United States of America.

SMOKING EXACERBATES ARTHRITIS SYMPTOMS

Smoking is hazardous not only for the diseases that it actually causes, such as lung cancer, but for the fact that virtually every disease and disorder is made worse by smoking. Arthritis is no exception to this. Tobacco contains toxic substances and smoking subverts up to about 15 per cent of the body's oxygen supply. This means that regeneration of damaged tissue takes longer and pain and fatigue is greater in arthritis sufferers who smoke than in those who do not.

In September 1997 the *Annals of the Rheumatic Diseases* published a report to the effect that smoking increases the severity of rheumatoid arthritis. The University of Iowa College of Medicine researchers who studied the severity of the disease in more than 300 patients report that smoking is a significant, modifiable risk factor for the severity of rheumatoid arthritis. Their study is the first to observe the effect of smoking on arthritis sufferers.

As we know, rheumatoid arthritis causes chronic inflammation and degeneration of the joints, typically those in the fingers, hands, feet, ankles, knees and shoulders. The condition is usually diagnosed by the presence of swollen joints, by X-rays that reveal erosion around the affected joints and by the presence of antibodies in the blood known as rheumatoid factor.

In the study, University of Iowa researchers evaluated 336 patients who had first visited the University of Iowa rheumatology or orthopaedics clinics between 1985 and 1992. Patients were asked about their rheumatoid arthritis, use of medication and other health factors, lifestyle and smoking habits. The patients also received blood tests, clinical evaluations and X-rays of their hands to measure the amount of bone erosion in those areas.

After adjusting for known risk factors for rheumatoid arthritis, such as age and gender, the University of Iowa team found that the patients who had smoked in the past or were current smokers were more likely to have high levels of rheumatoid factor and were at an increased risk for bone erosion. Moreover, those who had smoked for more than 25 years had three times the rheumatoid factor and bone erosion risks of non-smokers.

Smoking can cause abnormalities in the immune system of rheumatoid arthritis patients both in the lung as well as other parts of the body. Smoking increases a person's white blood cell count and heavy smoking can cause abnormalities in immune system cells that may increase risk of infection. Smoking compromises the activities of the immune system throughout the body and the authors of the study suggest that it may be more important in the initiation of erosive disease than in perpetuating the process.

GIVING UP SMOKING

Giving up smoking is the single most important step – far outweighing *any* other measure – that you can take to improve your health and this is even more so the case for arthritis sufferers.

There is only one way to give up smoking and that is to stop, having made the decision that that is what you really want to do. Withdrawal symptoms can be successfully relieved with nicotine chewing gum, nicotine skin patches or a nicotine inhaler.

Focus for the first few weeks on activities in which it would be difficult to smoke – such as cinema, theatre, swimming, exercise – and avoid any smoking friends if you can and the pub.

DRINKING ALCOHOL

Any food or drink that is acidic or fermented may worsen your arthritis symptoms.

Gout has long been associated with drinking alcohol and those with this condition should avoid it. Gout is caused by crystals that accumulate in the joints and these are caused by higher than normal levels of a substance known as uric acid. Some of the body's uric acid is excreted in sweat and some by passing into the digestive system where it meets bacteria that are capable of breaking it down. Most of the body's uric acid passes through the kidneys and is excreted in the urine. Any damage to the kidneys can interfere with their ability to get rid of uric acid.

Alcohol is well known to have adverse effects on the liver and the kidneys, the chief organs for the elimination of waste products. Toxic products therefore remain for longer in the body than they would if you were not drinking alcohol.

The more alcohol you drink, the more lactic acid you will produce in your blood. Lactic acid, in turn, is known to affect the kidneys and to make them less efficient at eliminating uric acid.

While alcohol is well known for its association with gout, alcohol – other than social drinking now and again – is also not advised in any arthritis condition. Heavy drinking and binge drinking are certain to exacerbate your symptoms and at the same time to reduce your ability to cope with the disease by causing fatigue and irritability.

The sparing use of alcohol in cooking is acceptable as some of the alcohol content will probably be burned off, leaving only the flavour of the drink and, in combination with food, alcohol is less toxic to the body in any case.

OTHER DRUGS

It is important that your family doctor is aware of all the drugs that you are taking, both prescription and over-the-counter drugs, so that you can be advised in the case of one drug reacting against another.

As for illegal drugs, it is well known that cannabis possesses analgesic (pain-killing) effects and some people therefore advocate its use in painful long-term conditions such as arthritis. However, cannabis remains illegal in most countries of the world and therefore poses risks to the user and to the supplier.

Chapter 9

Where You Live

We cannot always choose where we live but what we can do is observe any of those factors that may be detrimental to those of us who suffer with arthritis and compensate in other ways. We can, for example, pay even more careful attention to diet, make sure that we do enough exercise, get good-quality sleep and do our best to reduce our stress levels.

For those of us who are lucky enough to be able to choose where we live, the following are the factors to be borne in mind:

- ☐ Damp, rainy areas.
- ☐ Low-lying areas.
- ☐ Cold climate.
- ☐ Quality of water.
- ☐ Electricity pylons.
- ☐ Mobile phone masts.
- ☐ Pollution – from traffic, from industrial sites.

DAMP AND COLD

Both of these weather conditions tend to exacerbate arthritic disorders. You yourself may have noticed that your arthritis does not bother you as much once the weather is dry and sunny. Hilly areas, rather than low-lying areas, also favour the arthritis sufferer. A good breeze seems to blow away those aches and pains.

A couple of weeks' winter holiday in the sun – taken sometime in the months from November through to early March – can do much to alleviate joint stiffness.

A practical alternative to a winter's holiday is the weekly use of a sunbed, provided of course that you observe the safety conditions.

Many arthritis sufferers swear by this, saying that they feel wonderfully flexible after their weekly sunbed.

QUALITY OF WATER

Water is essential to the healthy functioning of the body. If you are lucky enough to live in an area where the water is of good quality and taste, make the most of it. If not, you may consider it best to buy bottled natural spring water (not carbonated) water. Fizzy water has no health benefits and is not particularly good for those with digestion problems.

ELECTRICITY PYLONS AND MOBILE PHONE MASTS

We still do not know enough about these hazards and whether or not they are truly injurious to health.

Many people believe that living in proximity to electricity pylons may prove carcinogenic.

Some experts believe that prolonged use of mobile phones and living in proximity to mobile phone masts are injurious to health.

Until we have conclusive scientific evidence, it would be wise to choose not to live near these hazards. If, however, you do and you cannot move, then do your best to mitigate any possible ill effects by paying the best attention to your health in all the other ways that you can.

POLLUTION

Emissions from traffic and from industrial sites are an inevitable part of modern life. However, we can choose to live in areas where pollution levels are lower or in areas of high ground where pollution will clear more quickly than it does in valleys and low-lying areas.

We can also do our best to offset the hazards of pollution and the ill effects that it may exert on our bodies by, once again, redressing the balance by paying close attention to all the other aspects of our health. These include good diet, regular sleep and exercise and keeping stresses to a workable minimum. Giving up smoking is particularly important for arthritis sufferers, too (*see Chapter 8*).

Part III: The Natural Therapies

Chapter 10

Acupressure and Acupuncture

Acupuncturists treat more patients with arthritis and back pain than any other complaint. Both osteoarthritis and rheumatoid arthritis have been found to respond well to acupuncture. Acupuncturists usually find that the treatment is more successful in less severe cases of arthritis, before the condition has become chronic with well-established degenerative changes that cause both restricted movement and severe pain. Acupuncture cannot cure arthritis but what it can do is alleviate the pain for longer and longer periods with each successive treatment.

Patients are treated by inserting very thin, hair-like needles into the skin at particular points. The acupuncture points lie along what are known as meridians, or invisible energy channels. Each of these 14 channels is believed to be connected to one of the internal organs, after which the relevant meridian is named.

It is believed in traditional Chinese medicine that our life forces, our energy, flows along the meridians. The life force, known as chi, comprises two principal components: yin and yang. The balance of yin and yang is crucial to a well-balanced mind and healthy body. Yin, the female life force, is traditionally believed to be passive and peaceful. Yang, the male force, is thought to be aggressive and confrontational. While yin represents dark, cold, moisture and swelling, yang represents light, heat, dryness and tautness. And while yin represents rest, earth, inwardness and water, yang represents activity, heaven, expansion and fire. Any imbalance between yin and yang is considered, in Chinese medicine, to cause disease and disorders.

Because it is believed that our energy flows along the meridians, and because disease represents an imbalance of our life forces, acupuncturists seek to release these blockages by freeing, or unblocking, the meridians in order to restore the movement of energy once more along the meridians. This is done by stimulating the acupuncture points.

There are believed to be up to 1,000 acupuncture points. Traditionally, it was believed that there were 365, one for each day of the year. Most acupuncturists in modern practice use no more than 200 points and some use fewer than this.

Acupuncture has been practised for thousands of years as one element of orthodox Chinese medicine. It is used to cure disease and to relieve pain. It has been used for analgesia during childbirth and surgical operations have been carried out under anaesthesia by acupuncture. This much is well-documented and cannot be disputed. Clearly, acupuncture works.

Some experts believe that the stimulation of the acupuncture points (by hair-like needles in acupuncture or by fingertip pressure in acupressure) leads to the release of endorphins, the pleasure and pain-killing hormones, and encephalins, which dull the senses, into the bloodstream and thus relieves pain. It is maintained that when the acupuncture needle is inserted, a nerve impulse is directed to the spinal column, thus releasing the endorphins.

Other experts subscribe to the gate theory of pain. This claims that pain impulses can be regulated by a gate along the pathways of the nervous system and that certain nerve fibres, when stimulated by acupuncture or acupressure, close the gate and thus shut off the pain.

Acupuncture is now used in orthodox pain clinics all over Great Britain as part of the National Health Service. Many doctors subscribe to its effectiveness, without understanding its mechanisms.

THE CONSULTATION

When you visit an acupuncturist for the first time, they will take a detailed medical and life history and will ask you questions about your lifestyle, your diet, what sort of exercise you do, your sleep patterns and your stress levels.

The acupuncturist will treat you according to the ancient rules of Chinese diagnosis. Your tongue, skin colouring and condition, your hair, posture and general air of well-being will all be noted, along with the sound of your breathing and your voice.

The acupuncturist will also use pulse diagnosis in order to determine how best to treat you. This enables the practitioner to gauge the state of energy in the meridians simply by taking your radial artery pulse at the wrist.

Once the acupuncturist has ascertained the full picture of your state of health, they will carefully insert needles into the acupuncture points at certain places on your body.

The insertion of the needles is usually quick, painless and bloodless. They are inserted to a depth of about 6-12mm and then rotated gently between finger and thumb to draw or disperse energy from the acupuncture point. You may experience a slight numbness or a tingling sensation. The acupuncturist may use only one or two needles and as many as a dozen or more. The needles are left in place for anything from a few minutes to more than half an hour.

The arthritis sufferer may feel some relief from pain with one visit, but it is more likely to take several visits, maybe half a dozen before a real benefit is perceived. It may also be that you will need to continue with acupuncture sessions for the relief of pain, as you may find that any relief is not long-lasting.

AT HOME

Although you cannot practise acupuncture on yourself, you can make use of the knowledge you gain during your visit to an acupuncturist by applying acupressure. To do this, you simply massage those points that afford you the best relief in acupuncture sessions with your fingertips. This is known as acupressure. Ask your acupuncturist how best to do this and which points to concentrate upon.

Some acupuncturists leave one or two needles in place which enables you to twiddle the needles whenever you have serious pain. Ask your acupuncturist if this is possible in your particular case.

Chapter 11

Alexander Technique

The technique was developed by F. Matthias Alexander, an Australian actor who earned his living in the late nineteenth century by declaiming orations and soliloquies from the classics.

One day he unaccountably lost his voice. Alexander consulted doctor after doctor, none of whom seemed able to help, or to discover any reason for the disability. So, Alexander decided to help himself. With the aid of specially positioned mirrors, he watched himself declaiming. Alexander observed that when he started to speak, he had a tendency to pull his head back and downwards, and he became convinced that this was the reason that he kept losing his voice.

Alexander concluded that it was not possible to separate mind, body and emotions, as all worked together. This concept, then revolutionary, became one of the main tenets of the Alexander philosophy.

Alexander also came to realise that whatever one did with one part of the body inevitably affected other areas, and that there was no such thing as an isolated body action. By dint of constant repetition, certain actions eventually would become ingrained and unconscious.

We slump in chairs, we put too much energy into mundane tasks such as washing-up, and we walk with round shoulders. In time, these habits become so ingrained that we cannot change them without a tremendous, conscious effort. Many bad physical habits, Alexander postulated, are initially caused by the mental or emotional problems of stress, tension and fear.

Alexander believed that many physical illnesses, including arthritis, are the result of long years of holding and using our bodies in wrong ways. Arthritis is a good example of years of wrong usage which eventually leads to pain, disability and sometimes deformity. The only solution is to unlearn the bad habits, bring them back into conscious awareness, and teach the body new, good habits.

Alexander believed that in order to stay well and healthy we must concentrate above all on the 'use of the self' as he put it, being aware always of how we sit, stand, move and generally conduct ourselves physically. Most people perform daily actions unconsciously, unaware that they may be damaging their bodies.

The most important part of the body, said Alexander, is the spine, as this is where primary control rests. Whatever happens in the spine affects the rest of the body: bones, joints, internal organs, digestion, as they all connect to the spine directly or indirectly. In order to do its job properly, the spine must be lengthened. When the spine is continually shortened, such as when slumping and slouching, undue strain is put on all the limbs and organs of the body.

Alexander believed that all diseases and illnesses are manifestations of a lack of harmony in the human system, and that many medical conditions have their root-cause in mental or emotional stress. Alexander observed that it is difficult to work on the mind alone. If you try to work only on the mind, without attending to the body, there is a danger that the problem will be masked rather than cured. As mental distress tends to be held and remembered in the body, close attention has to be paid to what has happened to the body to see what damage can be corrected.

Although the Technique benefits the mind and the mental outlook, as it paves the way for a more positive approach to life, Alexander teachers work mainly on the body, and concentrate on improving posture. Once this is corrected, they believe, good health and a positive attitude will follow.

It may seem that all you do at an Alexander session is to learn to sit, stand and lie in perfect symmetry. However, the lessons that you learn are not initially easy to put into practice in everyday life. Years and decades of wrong use take time, effort and dedication to correct. The emphasis at Alexander lessons is always on unlearning, rather than learning. You have to learn to 'unsit' and 'unstand' and to take your time in performing these movements, rather than just doing them without thought.

You are asked to wear loose-fitting, easy garments, such as a tracksuit and sweatshirt. Your Alexander teacher will ask you to sit, stand and lie down, and as you do so they will observe you closely, noting any tensions, strains and asymmetries. At your first lesson, the technique will be briefly explained to you, and you will be asked for a full medical history and questioned about your general health.

After about 15 minutes of consultation, you will be asked to lie on a table rather like a massage table, with your knees bent, and your head supported. This is to enable you to lie with a perfectly flat spine on the table.

The teacher will then test muscles and joints, and ask you to sit and stand in certain positions. They will then demonstrate the correct Alexander way of sitting and standing. You will probably be given some simple postures to practise between consultations. As time goes on, you will begin to recognise when your body is out of alignment, and be able to give yourself the instructions for correct usage and posture.

Chapter 12

Aromatherapy

An aromatherapy massage with a professional therapist can be exceptionally relaxing and at the same time alleviate some of your arthritis symptoms. You can, alternatively, treat yourself at home.

The power of certain essential oils to relieve arthritis was discovered by accident as a side-effect of treatment with plant essences. Austrian biochemist Marguerite Mary, who practised mainly in France, was one of the first therapists to use aromatherapy as a holistic mind and body treatment. Her work was inspired by Renee, a chemist, who had in the 1920s rediscovered the powerful antiseptic properties of certain aromatic plants.

The ancient Egyptians, with their love of sensuality and rich perfumes, are usually regarded as the founders of aromatherapy. They used aromatic oils for massage, healing and embalming. Egyptian mummies owe their extraordinary preservation to the powers of plant essences. Archaeologists have identified cedarwood and myrrh aromas lingering in the bandages of mummies that are 3,000 years old.

Many centuries later, it is now well-recognised that certain essential oils can bring about dramatic improvements in arthritic pain.

Essential oils are volatile, aromatic liquid components of strong-smelling plants. The liquids may be found in the petals (as with roses), leaves (eucalyptus, bay), wood (sandalwood), or bark, fruit (lemon, orange), seeds (caraway, black pepper), roots (sassafras), rhizomes (ginger) or resin (pine).

The orange tree yields aromatic essences from its blossom, its leaves and the fruit. Lavender produces aromatic oils from both its flowers and its leaves.

Essential oils promote the body's own natural healing mechanisms.

They penetrate the skin, entering the bloodstream, and act directly on the central nervous system. Different oils have different qualities. The oils are highly concentrated and a little lasts for a long time.

Essential oils can ease arthritis pain by calming inflammation and lessening pain. They can also reduce muscle tension. Certain oils have the power to help alleviate anxiety, depression and anger, all of which can be associated with the pain and immobility that arthritis brings.

The following oils and essences have been found helpful to relieve the pain and immobility of arthritis:

- ☐ Black pepper.
- ☐ Chamomile.
- ☐ Clove.
- ☐ Coriander.
- ☐ Cypress.
- ☐ Frankincense.
- ☐ Juniper.
- ☐ Lavender.
- ☐ Lemon.
- ☐ Sweet marjoram.
- ☐ Sage.
- ☐ Sweet thyme.

Aromatherapy oils for medicinal purposes come in very small dark brown or blue bottles with rubber stoppers. The oils must always be mixed with a suitable carrier oil, such as olive, sunflower or soya, before use and never used directly on skin. As the oils are extremely volatile, the stopper must always be firmly replaced. Aromatherapy treatments which are ready mixed and can be used directly on the skin are sold in large bottles and are labelled Massage Oil.

Here are some self-help aromatherapy treatments you can try for arthritis at home:

1. Dip a small towel in a basin containing very hot water, mixed with 15 ml (one tablespoonful) cider vinegar, two drops each of pine and cypress oils, and one drop of lavender oil. Apply this compress morning and night to the affected areas. Follow with an application of olive or nut oil and keep the areas warm.

2. Using a mild shampoo as a base, make up an emulsion containing one drop each of pine, juniper and cypress oils. Add this to a bath when running the hot water, and lie in it as long as possible. Afterwards, wrap yourself in a warm towelling dressing gown and rest on your bed for 10 minutes.

3. Pimento Massage Oil: this oil is very warming, and can thus help to relieve the pain of arthritis:

You will need:

10 ml (2 teaspoonsful) soya oil.

2 drops wheatgerm oil.

3 drops pimento oil.

Mix all together and apply to affected areas. Massage in well, then cover with a hot compress. You can apply neat soya oil to the skin afterwards, as it may be tender.

Some complementary therapists believe that arthritis is caused by a build-up of toxins in the body. They will suggest therefore that you use oils with a cleansing and detoxifying effect on the body. These include:

☐ Bergamot.
☐ Camomile.
☐ Cypress.
☐ Eucalyptus.
☐ Fennel.
☐ Geranium.
☐ Jasmine.
☐ Juniper.
☐ Lavender.
☐ Lemon.
☐ Neroli.
☐ Orange.
☐ Peppermint.
☐ Pine.
☐ Rose.
☐ Rosemary.
☐ Tea tree.

Don'ts

- ☐ Don't use homoeopathic remedies at the same time as aromatherapy oils.
- ☐ Don't use any oils that have toxic properties: armoise, arnica, baldo leaf, bitter almond, calamus, horseradish, jaborandi, leaf mustard, pennyroyal, rue, sassafras, savin, southernwood, tansy, thuja, wintergreen, wormwood.
- ☐ If you are pregnant or intending to be so, don't use any of the above, or angelica, aniseed and oregano. Be sure to consult a trained aromatherapist to help you make your choice of oils.
- ☐ Never buy cheap oils. Look for products that are described as Pure Essential Oil, not any labelled simply aromatherapy oil.

As with all arthritis treatments, aromatherapy helps some people more than others. Essential oils work best in conjunction with a healthy diet and a generally holistic, healthy regime (*see Naturopathy*).

Chapter 13

Chiropractic and Osteopathy

Chiropractic is more common in the States while osteopathy is more commonly practised in the UK. Both are techniques for manipulating the joints to help them function smoothly.

The principles of both techniques hold that the spine is the chief source of good health and that if you are able to heal the spine the rest of the body will respond positively.

Osteopaths and chiropractors use their manipulative abilities to bring relief of pain and to restore mobility to stiff and painful joints.

Osteopathy and chiropractic are suitable for osteoarthritis and wear and tear conditions of the spine but less so for rheumatoid arthritis and other forms of inflammatory arthritis.

Osteopaths and chiropractors can often help to relieve the symptoms of arthritis but, in common with doctors and other practitioners, they cannot cure it.

For sufferers of severe arthritis, instant relief from pain and stiffness is a bonus, but, usually, arthritic joints will stiffen again in time. Neither osteopathy nor chiropractic can reduce inflammation and nor can they prevent waste matter accumulating in the joints.

THE CONSULTATION

The osteopath or chiropractor will take a detailed case history from you, which includes asking you about your medical history and current lifestyle. Treatment sessions generally last for about an hour and up to six treatments will usually be indicated, depending upon the severity of your arthritis.

Osteopaths and chiropractors believe that the secret of their treatment is interspersing manipulative therapy with periods of rest to give the body its best chance of healing itself. After your treatment you will be given advice on how best to rest your joints.

One of the differences between chiropractors and osteopaths is the chiropractor's use of X-rays which osteopaths do not take.

Chiropractic involves pushing, pulling and levering muscle against bone. The number of sessions will depend, as it does with the osteopath, on the severity of the problem. You may experience some discomfort but nothing very painful.

Chapter 14

Colour Therapy

Colour therapists believe that colour not only affects our moods and feelings, but also affects the physical health and well-being of our bodies. We all know that a bright, sunny day can improve our spirits. A dark, dingy room is often depressing. The warmth of red cheers us through the winter.

Because colour therapy is such a gentle therapy, it is ideally suited to people with severe arthritis and any form of inflammatory arthritis. If colour affects our moods and emotions, colour, it is thought, must have some impact on our immune system, and, therefore, in turn, our health.

Archaeologists have discovered that the ancient Egyptians had special rooms built into their temples to be used for colour healing. In India, colour continues to be used as a therapy with the use of gemstones and Ayurvedic medicine. Each colour has long held its own religious significance. Later, the four humours, one of the theories of early medicine, were each assigned colours (red blood, black bile, yellow bile and white phlegm).

The body, according to the principles of colour therapy, absorbs colour in the form of electromagnetic components of light and then gives out its own aura of electromagnetism as a pattern of vibrations which can be discerned by a skilled colour therapist. A healthy body gives out a balanced pattern of vibrations, while an unhealthy body produces an unbalanced one.

The aim of the colour therapist is to administer the colour or colours that the sick person lacks, in order to restore the colour balance.

The human aura is ovoid in shape and made up of seven layers, the first of these being the physical body. Each of these layers interpenetrates others and is filled with ever-changing colours. These changes depend on our state of health and our mood. When we become angry, for example, our aura turns a murky red, and when we are envious it takes on a dark shade of green.

Disease manifests itself first in the aura and can be seen as a grey mass of accumulated energy. If this is not resolved, it will manifest itself as a symptom in the physical body. When treating a person with colour therapy, the aim is to disperse this accumulated mass of stagnant energy by reintroducing the colour frequency into the physical body and aura.

The ten colours most frequently used are red, orange, gold, yellow, green, turquoise, blue, indigo, violet and magenta. Yellow is sometimes used to treat arthritis.

Colour treatment can be administered either through a colour therapy instrument, which uses stained glass for filters or through contact healing. Contact healing involves the therapist allowing their body to be the instrument through which colour is channelled to the patient.

The most important function within the human body is the transference of life energy or prana. (This Indian word is Chi in Chinese and ki in Japanese.) Prana is absorbed into the body in many ways, including through the breath and through the food we eat. Prana vitalises the etheric layer of the aura which surrounds and interpenetrates with the physical body.

THE CONSULTATION

The colour therapist will take a detailed medical and life history from you and ask you about your arthritis condition, your lifestyle, your diet and how you exercise.

The first part of the treatment involves making a colour-diagnosis spine chart. This will give the overall colour needed plus information on your general condition. The overall colour required normally takes the form of clothing for you to wear and decor which you can introduce into your home. The therapist may also work with crystals of different colours and coloured water.

The colour therapist will feel and work with your aura to disperse any energy blockages and then lay hands over your body to allow the appropriate colours to be channelled into it.

AT HOME

Once you know which colours are best for you, you can continue the treatment at home by applying clothes of that colour or by wearing a piece of silk or cotton of that colour. Natural fibres are used because synthetic fabrics restrict the aura. You can also incorporate favourable colours into your decor. Gemstones are also sometimes used in colour therapy.

Chapter 15

Herbal Medicine

While Eastern countries are excitedly adopting Western medical methods, an increasing number of Westerners are turning back to traditional herbal remedies. Although many laboratory-produced drugs owe their origins to herbal components, natural, traditional herbal remedies are now making a significant comeback and, with them, the ancient skills of medical herbalism.

Before the advent of laboratory-developed drugs, nearly all medicines in all cultures were herbal remedies and that remains so in some developing countries. Although Western scientific medicine is making fast inroads in countries such as India and China, it is still the case that 85 per cent of the population in both countries rely on traditional herbal remedies.

Herbalism is an ancient art with a modern twist. Whereas the herbalists of old relied mainly on folklore handed down from one generation to another, modern herbal practitioners have to undergo rigorous training at a recognised school of herbal medicine, and their training includes working with Oriental as well as Western herbs. Because of this they have a far wider choice of treatments than practitioners in earlier times. Now that there are thousands of therapeutic herbs available to modern therapists, almost any ailment can be treated with a specific herb or combination of herbs.

Some ancient herbal remedies have now been evaluated in modern clinical trials at leading teaching hospitals so that, at last, we can find out why and how they work.

If you are interested in using herbal remedies for arthritis, it is important that you consult with your orthodox doctor first. Unlike some of the other complementary therapies, herbalism is not always compatible with orthodox drugs. Some herbal treatments are strong, and some can exert a negative as well as a positive effect. Some herbs clash with some of the ingredients in orthodox medication.

Herbs work quite differently from pharmaceutical drugs. Fundamental to the herbalist's view is that plants are used to restore balance and harmony to the whole body, rather than simply treat symptoms. Because the whole plant, rather than its isolated chemicals, are used, there is less risk of overdose or adverse side-effects.

THE CONSULTATION

The herbalist will take a full case history, asking about your medical history, your general lifestyle, diet, exercise routine, work, and personal stresses.

The chosen herbal remedy may be combined with a diet created specially for you, some beneficial exercises and advice on ways to reduce stress and anxiety. As with other complementary treatments, modern herbal medicine is a holistic treatment, taking mind, body and emotions into account.

Herbal treatments can be prescribed in the form of pills, teas, tisane or tincture, ointment, infusion, drops, suppository, enema, herbal baths, poultice or syrup. You may be prescribed a mixture of different herbal essences which you burn and then inhale.

AT HOME

Herbal treatments tend to be slower-acting than laboratory drugs, and, as they have a gentler action, are useful for chronic complaints. In fact, for a number of intractable conditions, such as arthritis, eczema and asthma, herbal medicine is superseding orthodox medicine.

As with other treatments for arthritis, whether they are orthodox or complementary, there is nothing that can guarantee a cure or permanent remission from the condition. Herbal treatments can be very complicated, and they should be administered by a fully-trained medical herbalist.

Herbs are not always safe:

☐ If you experience side-effects, stop taking the remedy.

☐ Do not exceed the stated dose.
☐ Do not take for prolonged periods as it is not known whether or not it is safe to do so.
☐ Don't pick from the wild.
☐ Don't buy from abroad.

The following herbs have been found useful in the treatment of arthritis:

Meadowsweet is the herb most often prescribed for arthritis. It contains salicylic (aspirin-like) glycosides and has a potent anti-inflammatory action.

Devil's Claw is also an anti-inflammatory and, in scientific tests, has been compared favourably with phenylbutazone, a commonly prescribed anti-inflammatory drug.

Burdock may be used to deep cleanse the tissues, and celery seed stimulates the elimination of uric acid and is therefore especially useful in gout.

Cornsilk and *Horsetail* strengthen the kidneys, and *nettles* help to rid the body of excess harmful acids. *Sarsaparilla* detoxifies, and *Prickly Ash* is a circulatory

Your herbalist may also use Chinese herbs such as *Achyranthes*, for getting rid of dampness in the joints, *Angelica* and *Large-Leaf Gentian*.

Chapter 16

Homoeopathy

Homoeopathic remedies are made from plants, minerals, animals and some diseased matter. These go through a process of dilution and shaking known as potentisation, through which the substance's healing power is released and all harmful, toxic qualities are avoided. The remedy acts as a stimulant for the body to heal itself. All such remedies are available from homoeopaths, from homoeopathic pharmacies, and also from some large chemists.

Homoeopathic medicine is based on the theory that 'like cures like' and it has been used for over 200 years. It was formulated in 1796 by Samuel Hahnemann, a German doctor who had become disillusioned with the common practice of using toxic substances to heal people. He looked at conventional medicine and saw that it was based on the law of opposites. In other words, you use a medicine to make the body go into the opposite mode. For example, if you have a runny nose you would take a medicine to stop your nose from running. Conversely, in homoeopathy, if you choose a substance which in a healthy person would produce a runny nose, the person with a runny nose to whom it is administered would be cured.

Hahnemann discovered that when this so-called 'similar' substance was used – similar in its ability to produce a symptom and therefore able to stimulate the body's own healing system into stopping the symptom – people healed gently, and permanently.

As homoeopathy is an holistic form of healing there are no remedies for ailments, but rather for individuals who suffer particular symptoms in their own individual way. Their individuality is what leads the homoeopath to the appropriate remedy.

Central to the concept of homoeopathy is that the smaller the dose, the more potent it becomes. This idea, which conflicts with conventional medical belief, has proved one of the most difficult stumbling-blocks in homoeopathy's long struggle for mainstream acceptance.

The amount of 'active ingredient' in homoeopathic medicine is that which constitutes a curative effect without producing toxic or adverse side-effects. Thus, homoeopathy is never harmful. However, as it is such a delicate remedy, its effects can be negated by strong drugs, foods or smells.

As with most other forms of complementary treatment, homoeopathy is intended to stimulate the body's own self-healing mechanism and to work without adverse side-effects.

Many orthodox doctors consider that homoeopathic remedies are no more than placebo, as they contain no discernible active ingredients. However, homoeopathy is becoming more popular, and it is now not unusual to find that at least one GP in a health centre is also a qualified homoeopath.

There are now many homoeopathic remedies you can buy over the counter, from high street chemists, but, with a chronic condition such as arthritis, you would be well-advised to consult a qualified homoeopath.

As some homoeopathic doctors are also fully qualified in orthodox medicine, they can understand the arthritis from both points of view, and can recommend mainstream treatments if they feel that these are required.

As with the other complementary therapies, homoeopathy cannot treat structural damage that requires surgery. If you need a hip replacement, for example, homoeopathy cannot help. It cannot repair worn- out joints or correct bone deformities. However, the appropriate homoeopathic remedies can speed up healing times after surgery. They can also work as preventative treatment, and thus guard against future damage and deformity by arthritis.

THE CONSULTATION

At the initial consultation, you will be asked detailed questions about your arthritis. You will also be asked about your medical history from the time of your mother's pregnancy onwards, your lifestyle, your likes and dislikes in life and the regularity of your bodily functions. You will probably be asked about childhood illnesses. Homoeopaths consider that many chronic complaints have a strong genetic element, and are passed down through the generations.

You will be prescribed a suitable remedy or group of remedies which you can obtain from a homoeopathic chemist. Most modern homoeopathic remedies come in the form of lactose pills impregnated with a solution of the remedy. The pills are simply dissolved on the tongue: they have no particular taste. Some remedies are sold in solution form in small glass phials with screw tops, and a few are available as ointments.

TREATMENT

In the UK, homoeopathic remedies are available on the NHS, provided that they have been prescribed by a homoeopath who is also a practising general practitioner. In many countries, these remedies are available under health insurance schemes, provided that they are prescribed by a qualified physician.

While taking homoeopathic remedies, you may be advised to modify your lifestyle, as experience has found that the remedies do not mix with some substances. The efficacy of the remedies may be reduced or negated if, at the same time, you are smoking and drinking and taking a lot of tea, coffee and colas. You may be asked to avoid highly-perfumed toiletries, strong-smelling household cleaners, and some essential oils. Some aromatherapy oils fight with homoeopathic remedies.

Homoeopathic remedies are unlikely to interfere with any orthodox drugs you may be taking, although many of these, such as steroids, sleeping pills and anti-histamines, will block the effects of homoeopathic remedies, making them a waste of money.

If you would like to stop taking your orthodox drugs before trying a homoeopathic approach, you should consult with your family doctor first.

Always be sure to tell your homoeopath what orthodox drugs you have recently been taking.

There are a number of remedies that have been found to be effective in treating arthritis, including:

- ☐ Rhus. Tox, or Toxicodendrum (poison ivy).
- ☐ Bryonia (white or common bryony).
- ☐ Ruta (rue).
- ☐ Calc. Hypophos (calcium hypophosphate).

Rhus.Tox is the basic homoeopathic remedy for joints. It is recommended for the types of arthritis that get better with the application of heat and worse after sitting for long periods.

Bryonia is useful for very painful joint conditions that are made worse by the least movement, but improve after rest and the application of cold compresses.

Ruta is a useful general remedy.

Calc. Hypophos. is a useful general remedy for arthritis of the hands.

It should be noted that homoeopaths believe in prescribing for the individual rather than for the condition. A consultation is, therefore, recommended.

Chapter 17

Hydrotherapy

Water therapy can give enormous benefit and relief of all types of arthritis. When the body is immersed in water, there is less strain on the weight-bearing joints, and this gives a feeling of comfort and lightness of being. This happens with both cold and hot water. Professional hydrotherapy for arthritis, however, is carried out in a hot pool.

Hydrotherapy works in two distinct but related ways. Firstly, it gives instant relief of pain and a sense of increased well-being and, secondly, being immersed in water allows greater joint mobility for the time that you are in the water.

Hydrotherapy is almost always combined with gentle exercise when the water allows the joints to become more mobile. After the exercise session, more hydrotherapy encourages the joints and muscles to relax in a soothing, comforting way.

Relaxing in a hot bath is a form of hydrotherapy in itself, but there are now special hydrotherapy pools available for use by arthritis sufferers. These are hotter than ordinary swimming pools, and are staffed by physiotherapists or other healthcare professionals who are expert in treating this condition.

Hydrotherapy and exercise sessions should always be carried out under the supervision of a healthcare professional. Otherwise, there is a risk that the joints could be exercised beyond their natural capacity, and result in more harm than good.

It is important that the water should be at the correct temperature, as water that is too hot or too cold will not be beneficial and may have the effect of restricting mobility.

For this treatment, you need to book a session or course of sessions at a special hydrotherapy pool. Some spas and health farms have pools that are adapted for arthritis sufferers. Treatment in adapted pools or baths may be combined with a hot seaweed or mud wrap afterwards, to reduce inflammation still further.

You may consider going to a residential spa which has a proven record for arthritis relief. One of the most famous is that at the Dead Sea, where specialised clinics staffed by qualified doctors can treat arthritis in its many forms.

Many natural hot pools and sulphur pools in different parts of the world have specialised arthritis clinics attached to them, and more and more people are discovering that this natural relief can last far longer than the pain relief obtained with pills.

At some spas in the Czech Republic, where scientific research has been carried out with arthritis sufferers, it has been found that hydrotherapy treatment in natural hot pools can give complete pain relief for as long as a year.

You can treat yourself to hydrotherapy treatments at home. Dead Sea minerals, and those from other spas, are now available from chemists for home use. These cannot, by law, claim to treat arthritis, but many sufferers find them extremely effective.

Walking by the sea and swimming in the sea have long been known to be healthy and people with arthritis can benefit from this form of hydrotherapy as well.

Chapter 18

Massage

Massage is a sensual healing art to be enjoyed and to produce a sense of well-being as well as bringing about real physical benefits to arthritic joints and muscles.

All massage techniques involve kneading and stroking, but there are many different types of massage, ranging from very light stroking to hard pummelling which may, for some people, approach the threshold of pain.

Here are a few of the most popular massage methods:

☐ Swedish massage uses a routine of basic, firm strokes over the whole body.

☐ Lymphatic drainage massage is newer than Swedish massage and is highly specialised. This form of massage concentrates on stimulating the internal organs by activating the various lymphatic points on the body. The idea is to enable long-held toxic matter to be flushed from the liver, kidneys and colon.

☐ Medical massage, which was originally developed during the Second World War for amputees and others suffering from serious wounds, concentrates on relieving very severe pain.

Massage is an ancient healing method and there is a long tradition of its use in most cultures. Massage was probably used by the early Christians as an element of healing by the laying on of hands, but it was eventually condemned by churchmen as sinful, as it involved one person touching another. Massage as a healing tool suffered considerably, especially in the West, with the advent of scientific medicine.

The ancient art of massage was revived in the early nineteenth century in Sweden, where a Stockholm University student, Henri Peter

Ling, started to duplicate gymnastic techniques on the massage table, thus developing the first form of passive exercise.

Ling devised 47 positions and 800 movements, so that those not athletically gifted could enjoy similar physical benefits to professional athletes. At first, the Swedish medical establishment and the government rejected Ling's system, but he eventually obtained a licence in 1814 to practise therapeutic massage.

The practice quickly caught on at spas and health clinics, particularly in sports medicine. Until the 1960s and 70s therapeutic massage was restricted to athletes, gymnasts and dancers and the wealthy few who could afford to visit health farms and clinics.

The appeal of massage began to broaden during the hippy revolution of the late 1960s, when Californian therapists began to use different forms of massage in their bodywork. Initially, the idea was to help people to break down repressions and long-held inhibitions so that their true unrepressed selves could be released. Gradually, however, it was realised that massage had many therapeutic uses, and so the therapy came to be incorporated into medicine. Most pain clinics now offer massage.

Massage has now become so integrated into modern medicine that it constitutes part of British nurses' postgraduate training. In America, therapeutic touch is taught at many medical schools, and it has become a branch of medicine in its own right.

Massage can benefit arthritis sufferers in several ways. At the simplest level, there is the fact that gentle stroking over your whole body with aromatic oils makes you feel better. Massage can ease the physical aches and pains of arthritis. Therapeutic massage can penetrate knotty joints and muscles and tease them out, helping accumulated toxins to be flushed out from the body.

Therapeutic masseurs, especially when working with arthritis or other inflammatory conditions, must understand the nature of the condition or they could make the inflammation and wear and tear worse. Professional masseurs undergo rigorous training which includes a detailed knowledge of anatomy and physiology, some psychology, and training on how to deal with patients.

You should tell your masseur exactly what your condition is and where your worst aches and pains are. You should also let your doctor know that you are having massage. You should check with your doctor before signing up for any massage that includes very deep pressure or soft tissue manipulation. Your doctor may advise only light massage.

A massage session can either sedate or stimulate, depending on the type of strokes used. Although it is sometimes considered to be a gentle therapy, massage can sometimes be quite tough. You should let your masseur know immediately if you feel any undue pain, as this is a warning sign. The strokes used on someone with arthritis tend to be much lighter and gentler than those used on a firm, athletic body.

The different strokes:

☐ Effleurage denotes light stroking in the direction of the heart. Although light, this form of massage is quite firm. It does tickle.

☐ Pétrissage is firm friction stroking, with more pressure used than in effleurage.

☐ Kneading denotes rhythmic lifting and squeezing of flesh.

☐ Tapotement indicates light hacking, tapping or clapping over muscles and the more fleshy parts of the body.

☐ Touch refers to putting the hand over a part of the body, a technique that is used for very ill people.

☐ Vibration is rapid shaking and pulsating, and this is often done with a machine.

☐ Brushing indicates light movements, using just the fingertips. This can tickle, and is used either at the end of a massage, or for people whose medical condition cannot take much pressure.

☐ Nerve compression refers to firm pressure applied to relieve knots or pain at nerve points.

THE CONSULTATION

At your first session, your massage therapist will take a full medical history and ask you questions about your lifestyle, your diet and whether or not you exercise. You will then be asked to undress and lie down on the couch. The massage room should be warm. You will be covered with warm, dry towels. Only the part of your body currently being massaged will be exposed, and then covered again afterwards.

Most masseurs use aromatherapy oils, although some prefer baby oil or even talcum powder. Male masseurs are usually able to apply deeper pressure than women, and some people prefer the large hands of a masseur. In some clinics, you can get synchronised massage, where two people massage you at the same time for extra effect.

The session should last for about an hour, by which time you should feel pleasantly relaxed. You will be asked to lie on the massage couch for a few minutes before getting up to leave. It is a good idea to have your massage at a time you will not have to rush around immediately afterwards.

A weekly massage is recommended for maximum therapeutic effect.

Chapter 19

Meditation/Visualisation/Relaxation

People often think of techniques such as meditation, visualisation, relaxation and self-hypnosis, as exercises or therapies designed to achieve emotional and spiritual well-being. However, these techniques have a profound impact on our physical body as well as our mind.

As the solution to emotional and mental problems becomes clearer, inner tensions are relieved, the body's energy or Chi starts to flow freely once again and toxic build-up starts to disperse. Complaints such as the pain and stiffness of arthritis, headache, backache, for example, start to diminish.

MEDITATION

Imagine yourself on a beach on a clear, sunny day with a little breeze blowing. The sea air courses through your nose and mouth, down the oesophagus, into your respiratory system. Feel your lungs expelling the toxins of traffic-laden air and inhaling the fresh sea breezes.

Concentrate now on the fresh air and nothing else. Hold this focus for some 20 minutes, while keeping your body entirely relaxed. Allow yourself to feel the breath coming in and out of your body.

VISUALISATION

Lie down in a quiet, darkened room. Allow your entire body to relax, limb by limb. Stretch and relax your neck and shoulder muscles. Start to visualise, bit by bit, the tension and the toxins pouring out of your body. Imagine a reflexology treatment or foot massage releasing the tension through your feet and ankles.

Work upwards through the body so that your leg muscles are cleansed, your digestive system is purified, your lymphatic drainage system eliminates toxins, your skin excretes toxins as it helps to relax your entire body.

RELAXATION

Lie on your back in a quiet room and allow each muscle of your body to relax. Stretch out your ankles and relax them. Flex your shoulder muscles and let them go. Lengthen, then release your torso. Wiggle the fingers. Now just lie still for some 30 minutes. Empty the mind. Be sure not to fall asleep: relaxation is a semi-conscious state, not sleep!

SELF-HYPNOSIS

A couple of sessions with a hypnotherapist is the best way of learning self-hypnosis. Decide what it is that you would like to focus upon, with your hypnotherapist, and allow them to take you into a deep trance-like state. Successful hypnosis achieves a completely relaxed, light state, free of anxiety and tension.

Chapter 20

Naturopathy

The principal elements of naturopathy are fresh air and sunlight, exercise, rest, good nutrition, hygiene, relaxation and hydrotherapy (water therapy).

Naturopaths believe that what orthodox doctors regard as symptoms of disease are indications of the body's attempts to reject disease and to throw off the toxic accumulations – the poisoning – that an unhealthy way of life has produced. They further believe that the body has the power to heal itself provided that is properly treated and maintained. Naturopaths attempt to remove obstacles to the normal functioning of the body, such as stress, poor posture and bad diet, and apply treatments which will stimulate or promote natural functioning. In essence, therefore, naturopathy is the promotion of a healthy lifestyle.

Many naturopathic practitioners, clinics and residential centres use modern medical methods such as X-rays, laboratory tests and so on to assist their work, but the essential approach is to help the body back into equilibrium by harnessing all the cures and treatments found in nature.

Naturopaths have to undergo lengthy training which includes anatomy, physiology, microbiology, gynaecology, orthopaedics, clinical nutrition, psychology and iridology as a diagnostic tool. They also have to study natural therapies such as homoeopathy, herbal medicine, traditional Chinese medicine, hydrotherapy and manipulative techniques such as osteopathy.

This complex training means that naturopaths can offer a range of treatments which are tailored to your individual requirements.

There are three basic principles in naturopathy. These are:

89

1. Naturopathic practitioners work according to the belief that the body is continually trying to restore health and maintain equilibrium, and that all symptoms of pain and distress are attempts to do this. Thus, a naturopath would see the pain and inflammation of arthritis as attempts to return to health. The pain exists to alert you that there is something wrong, and inflammation occurs when the joints are trying to protect themselves against further harm.

2. The belief that the underlying cause of all disease is the unwanted accumulation of waste products, and the body's inability to dispose of these naturally and safely. This accumulation is caused by poor lifestyle habits, for example, poor diet, junk food, lack of exercise and lack of fresh air.

3. That the body itself contains all the wisdom and power to heal itself.

THE CONSULTATION

Expect a detailed medical and life history to be taken. In some cases, laboratory tests or X-rays may be ordered. The naturopath may diagnose your nutritional status by carrying out a blood test or hair-mineral analysis. After the initial consultation, your therapist will discuss the various possibilities for treatment with you, and arrive at the package that seems the most suitable for your individual condition.

When you visit a naturopath, you may be prescribed controlled fasting, massage, enemas or colonic irrigation to detoxify the system and help the body to start cleaning itself out. Enzyme therapy, which enables the body to absorb nutrients in food, may be recommended. Many arthritis sufferers are not able to make full use of the nutrients the body takes in, so they may be prescribed freeze-dried plant enzymes in supplement form. The most common of these are bromelain from pineapples and papain from papaya.

Some people with arthritis have a history of poor diet and this will usually have to be corrected first. Vitamins A and E are powerful antioxidants, and work to destroy the free radicals which accumulate to cause damage around the joints. Vitamin E, in particular, enhances the production of cartilage and reduces inflammation and destruction of joint tissue.

Therapeutics on offer vary from practitioner to practitioner, but they may include using light, water, ultrasound, electricity, heat and cold. There may be exercise techniques such as yoga or breathing techniques; chiropractic, reflexology or massage; biofeedback; and herbal or homoeopathic remedies. You will almost certainly be advised to cut down on tea, coffee, colas, alcohol, refined sugars and, possibly, wheat and dairy produce as well.

Chapter 21

Reflexology

Reflexology is based on the principles of a life force flowing through the body along energy channels. Some reflexologists believe that these channels are energy pathways, while others believe that they are the same as the meridians which form the basis of the principle of acupuncture.

Reflexology is based on the concept that every part of the body is connected by the pathways which end in reflex areas on the feet, the hands and the head. By working over these reflexes in a precise and systematic way and, by applying controlled pressure, the reflexologist stimulates the body to achieve its own natural state of wholeness and good health. Tension or congestion in any part of the body is mirrored in the corresponding reflex areas on the feet.

Reflexology has appeared in many different cultures, in one form or another, around the world for thousands of years. It was known over 5,000 years ago in China and some 4,000 years ago in Egypt. The practice of reflexology spread to Europe in the Dark Ages and forms of pressure point therapy were used in the Middle Ages.

Reflexology, or reflex zone therapy as it was sometimes known, again became popular in the 1930s in the United States and was introduced into the UK in the 1960s.

One of the underlying theories of reflexology holds that as our ancestors walked and ran barefoot over uneven ground so the nerve endings and reflex points on their feet were constantly being massaged and stimulated. Nowadays, we spend much of our time sitting down, and when we do walk it is usually on hard, flat surfaces, wearing thick-soled shoes to cushion our feet so that our feet are no longer massaged and stimulated. When women wear high heels, the balance of weight on the soles of the feet is altered, putting extra pressure on some areas and failing to stimulate others. Before long, gravity causes a build-up of waste products, which the body cannot eliminate, and a general stagnation of energy in the feet.

The human body has the ability to heal itself. Following illness, stress, disease, the body is in a state of imbalance, with vital energy pathways blocked, so preventing it from functioning properly. Reflexology is used to restore and maintain the body's natural equilibrium and encourage healing. While reflexology cannot cure arthritis, what it can do is alleviate chronic pain and raise your energy levels.

Reflexology is used for alleviating fatigue and pain and works well with other treatments. People who have been prescribed drugs, or other medical treatments, find that reflexology reduces or eliminates side-effects, and so enhances the benefits of orthodox medicine. After surgery, reflexology helps to stimulate the healing process so that recovery is quicker.

Great Britain's Association of Reflexologists believes that the therapy is likely to involve some or all of the following processes:

☐ Deep muscle relaxation and the relief of tension and stress.
☐ An improvement in cardiovascular and lymphatic circulation.
☐ Stimulation and inhibition of the transmission of nerve impulses to the brain, particularly those involving the autonomic nervous system.
☐ The reduction of pain through gate control (the gate theory of pain as described in *Part IV*) and stimulation of the production of endorphins.
☐ Stimulation of the key points on the acupuncture meridians.
☐ Effects on the body's electromagnetic field.
☐ The benefits of an hour's rest, stillness and quiet.
☐ The psychological benefits of an hour's personal attention and care.

THE CONSULTATION

The reflexologist will take a detailed medical and life history from you during your first visit. You will be asked to lie in a comfortable, reclining position, with the feet raised and shoes and socks removed. The reflexologist will examine your feet, noting their general appearance, temperature and colour.

The reflexologist will exert thumb pressure of varying strengths over the pressure points of the feet, concentrating on any tender areas. These tender areas indicate those parts of the body that are out of balance. Sessions usually last for about 50 minutes.

During a course of treatment, the body experiences a process of detoxification. This may manifest itself as aching joints, diarrhoea, increased need to urinate, feeling a little flu-ish, feeling cold. If any of these effects occur, they are a good sign and they will not last long.

AT HOME

You may be able to achieve some relief of pain by working some of the reflexology points.

You will probably benefit by walking barefoot as much as you can. Walking around the house will naturally massage and stimulate your reflexology points. If you walk barefoot outdoors on grass, sand, earth or smooth rocks, again, you will help to raise your body's energy levels and sense of well-being.

Chapter 22

T'ai Chi Ch'uan

The most appealing factor for the arthritis sufferer about the therapy of T'ai Chi is its ability to harmonise body and mind, to restore harmony to the systems of the body, to boost the immune system, to improve the circulation, to boost energy flow and to begin the process of eliminating toxins from the muscles and joints of the body. All this can be done in a peaceful, gentle fashion without imposing any strain on the body.

T'ai Chi is one of a group of martial arts which were developed in China and Japan. The others include Aikido, Chi Gung, Judo, Jujitsu, Karate, Kendo, Kung Fu, Tae Kwon Do. These techniques are balanced systems of physical and mental training which are used for achieving understanding of the self, expression through physical movement and self-defence. Today, these techniques are not used so much as martial arts but as part of a quest for improved health, both spiritual and physical.

The Chinese system of T'ai Chi is said to date back many centuries when a Taoist monk, Chang San Feng, invented the movements seen today after dreaming about a strange part fight, part dance between a snake and a bird. In the system of Tao religion, the bird represents universal consciousness, while the snake symbolises earthly consciousness or the renewal powers of nature on earth.

There are now some 128 traditional recognised postures which are said to express the blending of the eternal and the present, heaven and earth.

You will benefit most from the T'ai Chi therapy by learning the postures from a recognised teacher and you can choose to learn as many or as few postures as you like and as many as you personally feel able to cope with. Just 24 postures practised daily will be seen to produce a health benefit.

Each of the postures, including the repetitions, takes some 20 minutes to perform. You may be encouraged to learn the short form of some of the postures and these take only about five to ten minutes to perform each one. Once you have learned the postures, you will be able to practise T'ai Chi alone at home, in your garden or in a public space, just as the Chinese do.

Many advocates of T'ai Chi suggest that this therapy is at least as beneficial if not more so than yoga for arthritis sufferers in that T'ai Chi increases the oxygen flow to the blood, and opens out the joints of the body, especially the knees, alleviating inflammatory diseases such as arthritis. Relief from pain, always an important concern for the arthritis sufferer, is just one of the benefits that T'ai Chi offers.

You will be able to find out about T'ai Chi classes available in your neighbourhood from your local library, from your local council offices, health club, adult education centre and possibly through your health centre (family doctor's surgery).

Chapter 23

Yoga

Yoga, together with aromatherapy massage, is the best known and most widely practised of all the natural therapies. There are many different types of yoga and classes show a wide variation in technique, in skill and in power. For the arthritis sufferer, however, yoga must be practised gently, taking into account the stiffness and immobility of arthritic joints.

Yoga therapy for arthritis has existed for many decades and is now available at the Yoga Therapy Centre based at the Royal London Homoeopathic Centre in London. The Centre offers a specialised eight-week course specially designed for arthritis sufferers.

A distinction must be made between osteoarthritis, which affects mainly older people and is caused by wear and tear on the joints, and rheumatoid arthritis, which affects the whole body and can result in eye and heart problems as well as stiff, painful, inflamed joints.

People with arthritis tend not to work their joints more than they have to and as a result the joints become ever stiffer and more painful to move.

One of the main benefits of yoga for arthritis is that sufferers learn to work their joints, slowly and gradually, once again. Correct movement is accompanied by special yogic breathing and relaxation exercises.

Yoga improves the circulation and helps to prevent further accumulation of waste mater in the joints. Yoga also keeps muscles working and in so doing promotes drainage of toxins from the lymphatic system.

Your family doctor and health centre may have details of classes which you can attend and then continue with the postures at home on a daily basis. Stop if you experience any discomfort.

Part IV: Seeking Help

Chapter 24

Seeing your Doctor

In the first instance you will need to see your family doctor who can then refer you to a hospital specialist, such as a consultant rheumatologist and/or an orthopaedic surgeon.

Your family doctor can also refer you to other specialists such as an occupational therapist, a physiotherapist and to a number of support services (*see Chapter 25*).

The conventional treatments for arthritis include:

☐ Medication (see below).
☐ Losing weight, exercise (both covered in *Part II*).
☐ Electrical therapy (such as TENS) described in *Chapter 25*.
☐ Occupational therapy and physiotherapy (see below).
☐ Surgical options (see below).

MEDICATION

Painkillers

There are two main groups of painkillers: non-narcotic drugs like aspirin and paracetamol, and narcotic drugs like codeine and morphine. Most of the painkillers you can buy over the counter are of the non-narcotic type. Some, such as ibuprofen, are NSAIDs.

Many brand-name painkillers are made by combining aspirin with other non-narcotic drugs such as caffeine, or with mild narcotic drugs such as codeine. Paracetamol-codeine combinations, for example, have been found to be slightly better at reducing pain than paracetamol alone. But be careful about mixing different analgesics: by taking two different brands of painkillers you may exceed the recommended dose for one of the ingredients.

It is best to avoid alcohol when taking analgesics and long-term use of these drugs should be medically supervised. Because they mask pain, it is also important to avoid damaging or overusing a joint when taking them.

Aspirin *(acetyl salicylic acid, acid acetylsal or acetylsalicylicum)*

Aspirin relieves pain in body tissues such as muscles, ligaments and joints, particularly when it is associated with inflammation. Pain relief is fastest if soluble aspirin is taken, dissolved in water.

Aspirin may irritate the stomach and, if taken on a long-term basis to relieve inflammation as well as pain, may cause stomach ulcers. It is best taken with food and some of the side-effects may be avoided by taking a buffered or enteric coated form of the drug which is less irritating to the stomach.

Aspirin should not be taken to relieve the pain of gout as it can interfere with other drugs which may be prescribed. Because it reduces the speed at which blood clots, it should not be taken by people with clotting disorders, or five days before surgery. It is also possible to develop an allergy to aspirin.

Paracetamol *(acetoaminophen)*

Paracetamol is also an effective painkiller but it does not relieve inflammation. Although swelling and stiffness of joints, for example, do not respond to paracetamol, it is generally the recommended and preferred treatment for osteoarthritis because it has fewer side-effects than aspirin or NSAIDs. However, care must be taken not to exceed the maximum dose (stated on the packet) because an overdose may cause serious liver and kidney damage. Paracetamol does not cause stomach irritation and can be taken safely by people with stomach ulcers. However, if you are a regular moderate or heavy drinker, you may be more susceptible to the ill-effects of paracetamol on the liver and should take a lower dose or use a different painkiller.

Benoral *(benorylate)*

Benoral is a compound made by joining aspirin and paracetamol together chemically. It is split up in the liver, delivering a regular quantity of both drugs into the blood stream It is an effective painkiller which also relieves inflammation, making it useful in the treatment of arthritis.

Narcotic analgesics

These drugs are generally available on prescription only and include morphine, dihydrocodeine, co-proxamol (Distalgesic) and diamorphine. Some are very powerful and long-term use can lead to tolerance and dependence. Although such drugs are not routinely used for people with long-term rheumatic disorders, some may be prescribed to relieve moderate or severe pain. Side-effects can include nausea, vomiting, drowsiness, constipation and, occasionally, breathing difficulties.

NSAIDs

NSAIDs – non-steroidal anti-inflammatory drugs – reduce inflammation as well as pain. Their main role in the treatment of arthritis is to reduce inflammation in the joint linings, thereby reducing swelling and relieving pain and stiffness. If no inflammation is present, as is often the case in osteoarthritis, NSAIDs may have no advantage over analgesics. That said, they are used for many different types of arthritis, often with other drugs. This is because they provide relief from symptoms, but do not modify the course of the disease.

The most commonly prescribed NSAIDs are: indomethacin (Indocid), naproxen (Naprosyn), ibuprofen (Brufen/Nurofen), fenbufen (Lederfen), piroxicam (Feldene) and diclofenac (Voltarol).

Doctors usually start patients on a small dose, increasing this if necessary. If one type of NSAID does not work, the doctor may try another because the response of individuals varies. NSAIDs are usually taken by mouth as tablets or capsules, although many are available as a liquid suspension or suppository. Some are taken only once a day, particularly those in a slow release or 'retard' preparation. A single, large dose of this kind, taken at night, often helps to relieve early morning joint stiffness.

Anti-inflammatory drugs start to work quickly, usually within a few days, although it can take two to four weeks for them to reach high enough levels in the blood to affect inflammation. They do this by blocking the production of prostaglandins, which not only trigger the nerve endings to send off pain messages, but also increase the flow of blood to the site where there is damage, making it red and swollen. However, because prostaglandins are constantly made and rapidly destroyed by the body, inflammation is quickly re-established once you stop taking NSAIDs.

Two large studies agreed that the safest NSAID was ibuprofen, while mid-range (in terms of safety) came diclofenac, naproxen and indomethacin. If you need to take NSAIDs long-term, you can help to minimise any side-effects by making sure you take them with or after food (a proper meal, not just a biscuit) and you should take a full glass of fluid along with the medication. Keep your alcohol and caffeine intake to a minimum and do not smoke.

Another NSAID, meloxicam (Mobic), is more narrowly targeted on inflamed tissues and has a lower incidence of side-effects on the stomach and intestine. Meloxicam is more expensive, but may be a sensible choice for anyone who has stomach problems with NSAIDs.

Sometimes NSAIDs can be combined with other drugs to protect the stomach against side-effects. Arthrotec, for instance, is a single tablet with diclofenac on the inside and misoprostol on the outside. Misoprostol protects the stomach by mimicking a type of prostaglandin and the diclofenac is not released until the tablet has passed through the stomach.

NSAIDs are not generally recommended during pregnancy and some should not be taken while breast-feeding. They may also make asthma worse and other side-effects may include nausea, stomach and bowel upsets, heartburn, indigestion, allergic reactions such as rashes and wheeziness, fluid retention and, rarely, kidney damage or blood disorders.

Some NSAIDs are available without prescription but it is unwise to take more than one NSAID at a time and some patients should not take NSAIDs at all. In addition, some other drugs interact with NSAIDs. It is, therefore, important, to discuss things with your doctor before you self-medicate.

NSAIDs also come in the form of rub-in gels. The advantage of local application is that much of the drug goes to the place where it is needed, reducing irritation to the bowel or stomach. Rubbing a gel into the skin also helps dilate blood vessels and the warming effect and prolonged massage may also help relieve pain.

ANTI-RHEUMATOID DRUGS

These drugs are often called DMARDs – disease modifying anti-rheumatic drugs – and play a key role in the treatment of rheumatoid arthritis. They may also be used in some other rheumatic diseases, such as ankylosing spondylitis or psoriatic arthritis.

They lower disease activity and inflammation, thereby reducing pain, swelling and stiffness of joints and are often effective where anti-inflammatory drugs are not. However, they also have higher levels of toxicity than NSAIDs, with potentially more damaging side-effects. They tend to be slow-acting and it may take weeks or even months for the full benefit to be felt. If you do not respond to treatment with one of these drugs, or develop any side-effects, such as stomach upsets, your doctor may try one of the others. As they are not analgesics you may have to carry on with painkillers or anti-inflammatory drugs unless your doctor advises you not to. They should not be taken during pregnancy.

ANTI-MALARIALS

Hydroxychloroquine and chloroquine are used to treat malaria, but they are also effective for rheumatoid arthritis and systemic lupus erythematosus. Side-effects are uncommon but a few patients develop skin rashes, indigestion, diarrhoea, headaches or blurred vision.

The greatest concern for patients taking anti-malarials is the risk of high doses of the drug affecting the retina, causing permanent visual impairment. Some rheumatologists and ophthalmologists believe that after an initial check, patients on low doses do not need monitoring for eye abnormalities. Others disagree, arguing that even on 'safe' doses regular eye checks by a specialist are essential.

PENICILLAMINE

This drug must be taken on an empty stomach, at least one hour before food – and you should not take iron tablets within two hours of taking it, as these can stop the drug being absorbed. The drug can alter your sense of taste, but this side-effect usually goes away within a few weeks. More serious side-effects are those which affect the blood, kidneys, skin and sometimes muscle. If you develop any rash, infections, fever, bruising, bleeding or any new symptoms, you should see your doctor as soon as possible.

GOLD

Gold has been used to treat rheumatoid arthritis since the 1920s and can be given in the form of injections or taken by mouth. The injections of gold, **sodium aurothiomalate**, are often referred to as Myocrisin, the most common brand name. Your doctor may recommend a test dose, to make sure you do not have an immediate reaction. If all is well, injections are generally given once a week, either at your GP's surgery or at hospital. After some months, if you are benefiting from the injections, your doctor may be able to reduce their frequency to once a fortnight or once a month. The injections are given into a muscle, usually the buttock.

Gold can cause problems with the blood, kidneys or skin. Some of the side-effects can be picked up early by regular checks on your blood and urine. But if you develop a rash, mouth ulcers, altered taste, sore throat, fever, bruising, bleeding, breathlessness or any other symptoms, report them to your doctor as soon as possible.

Auranofin is an oral preparation and tends to be less effective than gold injections. Diarrhoea is the most common side-effect, but gold tablets can, like gold injections, cause problems with the blood, kidneys or skin, so regular monitoring of blood and urine is necessary and you should see your doctor if you develop any new symptoms such as those listed above.

Sulfasalazine

A combination of an antibiotic and aspirin, this drug is generally prescribed as Salazopyrin EN, a form of tablet which is specially coated so that it does not dissolve quickly in the stomach. It may cause fever, nausea, headache, dizziness, rashes, diarrhoea or abdominal pain. Any more serious side-effects on the blood or liver can be picked up early by regular blood checks. The drug is excreted in most body fluids so your urine may turn orange and soft contact lenses may be stained yellow. It also causes sperm counts to drop in men, but this drop in fertility is reversible on stopping the drug.

Methotrexate

Methotrexate is also used to treat rheumatoid arthritis and other types of rheumatic disease. It can take three to twelve weeks to produce noticeable benefits and carries the same kind of risks as the other immunosuppressant drugs. Because it can affect the blood count and can sometimes cause liver problems, your doctor will arrange regular blood checks while you are taking it. Some doctors prescribe folic acid tablets to be taken as well, as this can reduce the likelihood of side-effects.

IMMUNOSUPPRESSANTS

Because some types of arthritis – rheumatoid arthritis and lupus, for instance – belong to the family of autoimmune diseases, drugs which damp down the activity of the immune system may be used to treat some patients. All of them affect the body's natural defences and may produce side-effects, so they need careful monitoring. These drugs should not be taken during pregnancy or while you are breast-feeding and, as they may interact with other drugs, you should always let any doctor treating you know you are taking them. However, as they are not analgesics you may continue to need painkillers – but discuss this with your doctor before taking over-the-counter preparations.

The drugs include azathioprine, methotrexate, leflunomide, ciclosporin and cyclophosphamide.

STEROIDS

Steroids are manufactured versions of hormones produced naturally in the body. The steroids used in the treatment of arthritis, are corticosteroid drugs, which are derived from, or are synthetic variants of the natural corticosteroid hormones formed in the outer part of the adrenal glands. When present in large amounts, corticosteroids reduce inflammation and suppress immune responses. This is why they are used for patients with rheumatoid arthritis and other types of rheumatic disease.

Steroids were hailed as wonder drugs when they were first introduced, but it soon became clear that there were serious drawbacks to long-term use. Rheumatologists agree these drugs still have a role to play, but opinion remains divided as to exactly when and how they should be used.

Injections

Steroids can be given by injection into an inflamed joint, and can help with sudden flare-ups. Injecting a joint is called an intra-articular injection. Injecting near a joint is called a peri-articular or soft tissue injection. This may be done to reduce pain or inflammation if you have tennis elbow or a frozen shoulder, for instance. Commonly used steroids are hydrocortisone or prednisolone, although triamcinolone and methylprednisolone may be used for larger joints.

Injecting a steroid concentrates the drug in the relevant place and minimises the amount dispersed in the body, so side-effects are unlikely. Very occasionally patients notice a flare-up in their joint pain within the first 24 hours after the injection, but this usually settles by itself over the next couple of days. Very rarely infection might be introduced into the joint at the time of an injection, so if the joint becomes painful and hot, it is important to see a doctor at once.

Occasionally some thinning of the skin may occur at the injection site with peri-articular injections.

It is important to rest for at least 24 hours after an injection, even if the joint feels as good as new, especially if a weight-bearing joint such as the knee or ankle is injected.

Steroid tablets

Prednisolone is the most commonly prescribed steroid tablet for patients with rheumatoid arthritis and other rheumatic diseases and can be very effective in reducing inflammation. If you suffer from indigestion or are taking a high dose, your doctor may prescribe enteric-coated tablets.

The dose will depend on why prednisolone is being used and on your body weight. Often, a doctor will start a patient on a high dose and reduce this as symptoms improve. However, if a patient has been on steroids for a long time, it is important to make reductions slowly. The body has a sensitive system for regulating the amount of corticosteroids made by the adrenal glands. Taking oral steroids overrides this system and the body rapidly becomes dependent on the oral steroids. So it can be dangerous to stop taking steroids suddenly: even cutting down should be done slowly and under medical supervision. A doctor may decide that a patient should continue on a small maintenance dose indefinitely.

The longer you take prednisolone and the higher the dose, the more likely you are to have problems with side-effects. These include bloating, cramps, weight gain, a round 'moon' face, stretch marks, thinning of the skin. Cataracts can also occur. People on steroids are more prone to infections and illnesses. Muscles can become weak and wounds slow to heal. High doses can also affect blood pressure, diabetes, moods and sleep patterns. Long-term use can also cause osteoporosis. A doctor may try to minimise this risk by prescribing calcium supplements, hormone replacement therapy or other medication.

All of this may sound alarming, but untreated inflammatory disease also carries risks: it is a question of weighing up risks and benefits.

If you are on steroids

☐ Always carry a Steroid Card which records what you are on and how long you have been taking it. You might want to wear a MedicAlert bracelet. If you are unwell or are involved in an accident you will probably need extra steroids.

☐ Never stop taking your steroids unless advised by your doctor.

☐ If you are sick, have diarrhoea or can't take your tablets contact your doctor for advice.

EARLY TREATMENT IS VITAL

Not long ago there was some debate as to whether early, aggressive therapy made any difference to the outcome of patients with inflammatory arthritis, including rheumatoid arthritis. Treatment tended to be based on the idea of first- and second-line drugs, beginning with NSAIDs and progressing to DMARDs, such as gold, sulfasalazine and methotrexate. Most rheumatologists are now convinced that accurate diagnosis and appropriate intervention with drugs and physiotherapy in the early stage of the disease is crucial, because the longer inflammation lasts, the more damage is caused. This means patients are now more likely to be prescribed one or more disease modifying drugs early on. Doctors argue that once inflammation is suppressed, patients will not deteriorate and should actually improve. Patients also seem less likely to suffer side-effects from these drugs if they are treated sooner rather than later.

OCCUPATIONAL THERAPY

If you visit hospital with arthritis, or go to a clinic, use part of your time to discover how best to cope with any disability you have in hospital and subsequently at home so that you can maintain your normal occupations as far as possible. Occupational therapists will be able to recommend ways of doing things and gadgets that can help with this. You can derive much satisfaction and a sense of being in charge of your own life from adapting your home environment. Some ideas are described in this section and a therapist will recommend those that are particularly useful in your case. (*See also Chapter 25.*)

Your problems are likely to start with getting up in the morning. Occupational therapists are trained to advise and help with this. The clothes you choose can help enormously, with the emphasis being on things that are easy to slip on or off, so as to avoid fiddly finger movements and having to bend down to the level of your feet.

Slip-on shoes, zips with easy-to-hold pulls rather than buttons, Velcro fastenings and belts that hook rather than buckle all make life easier. You may invest in gadgets such as a long-handled shoehorn and a buttonhook to help do up small buttons. You may have to avoid clothes that are done up at the back.

Where you keep your clothes matters too. Bending down to pull open low, stiff drawers should be avoided as far as possible. So should cluttered pathways between the bed, bath or shower, chest of drawers and dressing table. Clothing should be stored in as open a way as possible – perhaps on open shelves behind a curtain.

Bathing and washing can be painful and difficult for someone suffering from arthritis. An occupational therapist can advise you on the best available aids for you. Rails on the bathroom wall are useful, and rails on the edge of the bath are vital as soon as getting in and out proves painful. A non-slip rubber mat on the bottom of the bath is a wise safety measure. Taps that have push up and down controls are easier than ones that have to be turned. A back-scrubbing strap is easier to use than a back brush. Put the soap somewhere where there is no risk of slipping on it.

If your fingers are even moderately affected, you may find using an ordinary toothbrush or razor difficult. Long handles can be fitted to toothbrushes. Electric razors may be easier and safer.

Getting on and off the lavatory seat can be a problem with painful knees, hips and weak legs. A higher toilet seat to reduce the distance you have to raise and lower yourself helps. It can be installed with the toilet or bought as an add-on. Armrests can be attached to the toilet and rails can be fitted to help you get up and down. It is important to have these aids properly fitted.

In the kitchen, you may need a variety of gadgets to make your life easier. You can buy a gadget to open jars, for example. Corkscrews should be the double-action type that avoid the need for hard gripping and back-wrenching pulling. Occupational therapists can advise on a range of aids for eating and drinking. Serrated knives help in cutting up food. High-friction plastic or rubber mats placed under the plates stop them slipping. Specially designed mugs and other utensils are also available. (*See Chapter 25.*)

PHYSIOTHERAPY

It is important that you avail yourself of the advice of your hospital's physiotherapist. Ask your family doctor for referral to a physiotherapist if you are not already in contact with one at the hospital. Your physiotherapist will be able to give you valuable advice on your own particular problems. They will help you with exercise problems, recurrent pain problems and any problems associated with managing your life at home.

SURGERY

Surgery is sometimes the only remaining option after all other treatments have proved inappropriate. In some cases the joint is completely replaced and, in others, one of the surgical procedures described below suffices.

Synovectomy

Synovectomy is the surgical removal of the synovium, the thin membrane that lines the normally fluid-filled joint capsule, the cavity where the ends of two bones meet in a joint. The operation is usually performed to treat cases of severely disabling rheumatoid arthritis that have failed to respond to other treatments, which may have included injections of corticosteroid drugs, non-steroidal anti-inflammatory drugs and other anti-rheumatic drugs.

Debridement

Debridement is mainly used for the treatment of conditions affecting the knee. It is used when the load-bearing surfaces and the lining of the joint have become rather worn or damaged, so that little bits tend to fall off, get into the joint and cause joint swelling.

Where there is a mechanical problem, such as a worn bearing surface, debridement can be useful. The majority of debridements today are performed with a telescope or arthroscope, using keyhole surgery.

Debridement is a holding operation carried out on slightly worn joints in order to postpone more serious surgery.

Osteotomy

Essentially, osteotomy means cutting a bone so that it can be put back in a different position; sometimes in the hip, often in the knee, frequently in the foot and rarely in other joints. It may also be performed after a fracture when bones have not healed in the right position, when a surgeon may choose to cut the bones so as to put them back in the correct position.

With the increasing use of joint replacements and a growing ability to correct abnormalities early without the use of bone surgery, osteotomy is being used less today, but it remains a valuable technique.

In the knee, osteotomy is used in an older age group, usually because the patient has been bow-legged. This results in more weight than should be the case being carried by one side of the joint, which may, consequently, become excessively worn. An orthopaedic surgeon can often solve the problem by breaking the shin bone, the tibia, taking a wedge out of it and joining it again, so that the weight is transferred from the worn side to the unworn side of the knee joint.

Like any broken leg, it will take four to six weeks to heal. The results of this operation in the short term are usually good, but hard to guarantee. The average duration of relief from symptoms is seven to ten years. After that an operation for the replacement of hip or knee joint is usually required.

Osteotomy is also performed on smaller joints. The most common such application is for the bones of the foot. The metatarsals, the bones between the ankle and the bases of the toes, sometimes drop down so that those people affected feel as if they are walking on stones around the base of their toes. The operation to correct this simply involves breaking or cutting the bones and resetting them, so the hard ends that have been pressing on the ground can ride up, removing the sensation of walking on pebbles.

Arthrodesis

This is the name given to any operation in which a joint is cut out altogether, and the cut ends of the bones that used to meet in the joint are fused together. This is an extremely effective though drastic way of getting rid of severe pain in a joint affected by arthritis – completely removing all diseased tissue and eliminating the possibility of further arthritis in that area.

Arthrodesis was very much the treatment of choice for many cases of rheumatoid and osteoarthritis in earlier days, when other surgical techniques were less developed than they are today. Today, arthrodesis is used only very rarely in severe osteoarthritis, in cases in which the pain is so severe and the crippling effect of the condition so considerable that the price paid in loss of mobility or freedom of movement is considered well worth paying.

The joint most commonly removed by arthrodesis today is the big toe joint, to get rid of a bunion, a form of osteoarthritis in which the joint is severely affected by wear and tear. Arthrodesis can make your walking a bit stiff and awkward, though most people become used to that.

Arthrodesis may be the best solution for rapidly progressive rheumatoid arthritis in a very young person, for whom it is too early to perform a joint replacement, or in an elderly patient whose first or possibly second joint replacement has failed, and for whom there is little or no chance of success with a further replacement.

Joint replacements

In a hip replacement the natural bone ball at the top of the femur is removed and a metal spike is driven deep into the femur, held in place by cement. The socket on the pelvis in which the ball naturally rotates is replaced by a socket made of very high-density polyethylene plastic.

This type of replacement has been one of the great surgical success stories of all time. As well as being fitted with confidence into people in their eighties and older, hip replacements are being fitted in younger and younger people because of the good quality of life they can provide. However, this means that, increasingly, the artificial joints are wearing out well before death, so there is a growing need for second joint replacements.

These continue to leave the person involved free from pain and much more mobile than they would be without the replacement. However, the second replacement is never as good as the first one. The second operation has to be performed on a patient who may be 15 years older and more frail and, therefore, that much less suitable to face the slight but real risks of any major surgery.

The consequence of this is that scientists and engineers are now engaged in trying to produce a hip replacement that will last substantially longer than those in use today.

An artificial hip joint, good as it is, is never as good as the natural joint. You will be told, for example, to avoid too much bending at the hips (squatting, sitting in low chairs, for example). You will also be told, and this is more difficult to remember, not to cross your legs because that can dislocate your new hip, which is not held in place as firmly as the natural one.

None of this should depress you, for the gains in this type of operation far outweigh any losses. One reason for the strong warnings that accompany a replacement hip is that people who receive one are often so pleased with the improvement in their quality of life, freedom of movement and absence of pain that they believe that they can do anything and expect too much from their new hip.

You will probably be able to drive a car again after four to six weeks, being careful not to bend your hips or raise your legs too much as you get in and out. You will be able to walk, swim (avoiding breaststroke because of the effort required by hips and knees) and ride a bicycle. You will need to avoid running and playing games on hard surfaces since this can jar your hip and overload the joint. Most kinds of moderate exercise, however, are good for you and your new hip is designed to cope with them.

Knee replacement is now almost as routinely successful and beneficial as hip replacement.

Rapid progress is being made at present with the design of new finger joint and ankle joint replacements.

Chapter 25

Living with Arthritis

Arthritis is a challenge, both physically and emotionally. But you can cope with it if you decide to take control, rather than let it control you. This means learning as much as possible about the condition, finding ways round physical limitations, being open with family and friends, and not setting goals which you cannot realistically achieve.

When you are first told you have arthritis you may feel a sense of shock, disbelief or helplessness, followed by a feeling of anger. When you realise that arthritis has become part of your life you may feel depressed. These emotions are perfectly normal and all part of the grieving process – you grieve for the person you once were and all the things you could once do. This grieving process is often necessary for you to accept change and get on with your life.

COPING WITH STRESS AND FATIGUE

Stress and fatigue can become part of the negative cycle of arthritis unless you positively avoid it. Recommended techniques include regular exercise, relaxation, saying 'No' so that you don't take on too much, getting enough rest, pacing yourself, keeping a good body posture, protecting your joints and getting enough sleep.

RELATIONSHIPS AND SEX

Everyone has a need for intimacy and security. If you work on having loving, honest relationships that allow you to express and satisfy your needs, you are less likely to have problems. If problems do arise, the best way to improve all aspects of a relationship, including sex, is to be honest and open. Cherish and pamper yourself so that you feel attractive.

Arthritis does not directly affect sexual functioning so it need not interfere with your love life. Enjoying sex means you feel pain less or forget about it altogether. Making love gently, at the right time for you, can have a healing effect. Talk to your partner, telling them what you like and what makes you feel good. Sex is a great stress-buster and great exercise. Enjoying making love with your partner boosts self-esteem and helps you stay in a positive frame of mind. Behaving in a loving way to your partner, and getting love in return, can help when you are feeling low. So be generous with hugs and kisses.

SELF-CONFIDENCE, SELF-ESTEEM AND A POSITIVE OUTLOOK

How you feel about yourself can have a profound effect on the level of pain you feel. When you have a painful, debilitating illness it is easy to lose confidence, self-esteem and a positive outlook. These are sapped still further if you can't work any longer or have difficulties in a relationship. You may become depressed, with symptoms of poor sleep, lack of appetite, and gloomy thoughts. But there are ways to boost your health, both psychological and physical. The key is Control, Commitment and Challenge – the three Cs. People who keep hold of positive self-esteem under stressful life circumstances feel:

☐ **In Control** of their lives (not helpless).

☐ **Committed** to their lives, in which they find meaning both at home and at work.

☐ **Challenged** by events (instead of threatened by them).

YOU SHOULD:

☐ Build up your self-esteem by doing creative things like painting, writing, sculpture, or singing, for example. These help you express yourself and give you a sense of achievement.

☐ Do things that make you feel happy and fulfilled. Do things positively, with purpose, in a way that makes you feel of value.

☐ Be kind to yourself. Look after yourself. Nourish and encourage yourself.

☐ Let out bleak feelings like resentment, anger, fear and grief.

115

☐ Visualise how you want your life to be. If you concentrate on positive images and aims, they are more likely to happen.
☐ Try to make a positive contribution to your community.
☐ See everything in life as an opportunity to grow and learn, accepting yourself and what is in your life. Forgive yourself for mistakes that you have made, learning what you can from them and moving on.
☐ Keep your sense of humour.

COUNSELLING

If you are suffering from the emotional effects of having arthritis – a negative self-image or depression – ask your family doctor to refer you to a counsellor or psychologist.

YOUR WORK

You have to be realistic. Go for jobs that fit in with your physical abilities and limitations. It is probably better to inform your employer that you have arthritis. That way, you are less likely to be asked to do things beyond your physical capabilities.

SELF-HELP GROUPS

Many people find it helpful, therapeutic and supportive to meet other people with arthritis at self-help groups. You can swap tips with other people, and everyone else understands the pain and frustrations. Self-help groups are often run by people who have arthritis themselves, so they understand the condition. Contact your local Arthritis Care branch or Young Arthritis Care.

MANAGING THE PAIN

One of the biggest challenges facing people with arthritis is pain. You may be in pain every single day and night. The degree of pain can vary; sometimes it's worse than at other times. However, there are many things besides drugs that can help ease the pain. What works for one person may not do the trick for another, so you may have to try out several methods.

PAIN IN ARTHRITIS

Some people describe pain like a burning or searing sensation. What makes you feel pain is inflammation in the joint areas causing swelling, redness, local heat and loss of movement. Damaged or worn joints can be painful, too. Both of these can lead to the pain of muscle strain caused by trying to protect the joints from painful movements. The hard part about pain is that it cannot be seen by other people. You sometimes have to endure crippling pain on your own. Left untreated, pain can sap your energy and leave you virtually unable to function. It can make you feel angry and full of self-pity. Acknowledge pain as a fact of life, but if you give in to pain it can have a destructive effect, affecting your mood, outlook, and relationships. If you are anxious, depressed, stressed, or fatigued the pain feels worse. If you are not careful, you can be caught in a vicious circle of pain, depression and stress which can interfere with your quality of life. But, when you learn to manage your pain, this is less likely to happen.

THE 'GATE' THEORY OF PAIN

There is a 'pain gate' in the spinal cord. When this 'gate' is closed, painful nerve signals are prevented from reaching the brain. The brain and spinal cord can release their own pain-relieving chemicals, called endorphins, which close the pain gate naturally. Endorphins can be released by exercise, massage, heat, cold, hydrotherapy, physiotherapy, sex and a positive attitude.

A POSITIVE ATTITUDE TO PAIN

A positive attitude means that you are less likely to lead a life that revolves round pain and illness. The occasional moan and groan is to be expected, but the more you get locked into pain the worse it can feel. Try and take your mind off the pain by doing the things that you really like. Enjoy humour, eat good food, do some exercise every day, go out with friends. Give yourself treats and have something to look forward to every day. Indulge yourself and go to bed each night in a good frame of mind.

PROTECTING YOUR JOINTS

Protecting your joints involves doing daily activities in ways that reduce stress on your joints.

- ☐ Become aware of your body positions and avoid activities that involve a tight grip or put too much pressure on your fingers. Avoid holding one position for too long.
- ☐ Use your largest and strongest joints and muscles for daily tasks wherever possible. Spread the weight of an object over many joints to reduce the stress on any one joint.
- ☐ Use aids and gadgets to make difficult tasks easier.
- ☐ Control your weight to avoid extra stress on your weight-bearing joints and further pain and joint damage.
- ☐ Ask for help when you need it. Don't suffer in silence.

SAVING ENERGY

- ☐ Listen to your body for signals that it needs to rest.
- ☐ Pace yourself, don't push yourself. If you overdo things it can lead to exhaustion and could cause a flare-up.
- ☐ Don't expend energy on things that don't matter. Try and find ways of doing things with the least energy expenditure.
- ☐ Find a healthy balance between activity and rest. Sit down when you can. Take breaks whenever you need them. Plan rest times to make sure that you take them. But don't rest too much as this can cause muscle stiffness.

NON-DRUG WAYS TO MANAGE PAIN

A self-help pain management programme can involve any of the following:

- ☐ **Heat.** Some people benefit from heat, while others find that it makes them more uncomfortable. The same applies to cold. Some find a combination of heat and cold in a single treatment works best.
- ☐ **Moist Heat.** Soak in a nice hot bath. Add oils or Epsom salts. There are several manufacturers of home-spa equipment which

are recommended for arthritis. You lie on a special mattress connected by a hose to a machine which blows air, making the water bubble. Put warm towels or hot packs where you need them. You should not do this for longer than 15 to 20 minutes, three times a day.

□ **Dry heat.** Heating pads can be used to warm painful areas. Some just need to be popped in a microwave oven to heat up. Electric blankets and mattress pads are very comforting. Flannelette sheets feel warmest against the skin. A hot-water bottle wrapped in a towel keeps selected parts of the body warm. Warming clothes on the radiator before you put them on can help. Deep heat massagers provide deep heat inside the joint but with no risk of burning the skin.

□ **Cold.** Like heat, cold helps relieve pain for some people but not others. Cold is especially good for the acute inflammation felt in the joints during a flare-up. Cold helps reduce swelling, lessens muscle spasms and numbs the pain. Buy a cold pack at the chemist's, or you can make your own by wrapping a damp cloth or towel around a bag of frozen vegetables. Apply for 10 to 15 minutes at a time. Do not use if you have poor circulation.

□ **Contrast bath.** A combined hot and cold treatment. You soak a hand or foot in warm water, then cold, then warm again.

□ **Hydrotherapy.** Water therapy can decrease pain and stiffness. Many health farms have warm spa baths and pools. These invigorate at the same time as relaxing you. Some hospital physiotherapy centres have warm hydrotherapy pools. Gentle exercises or aquarobics at your local swimming pool are also good hydrotherapy for arthritis.

□ **Massage and self-massage.** Massage involves massaging or kneading the muscles in a painful area to increase the blood flow and bring warmth. You may be able to do this yourself. If not, ask a partner or close friend, or find a professional masseur. Using an oil can help hands glide over the skin, and some people find that using a menthol gel provides a pleasing sensation that eases pain. If pain develops while having a massage, stop. Do not massage a joint that is already inflamed.

☐ **Deep heat rubs.** These block the sensation of pain and increase local blood flow in the skin.

☐ **Splints.** Splints rest the joint, reducing inflammation and pain.

☐ **TENS (transcutaneous electrical nerve stimulation).** TENS involves stimulation of the nerves by low-level electrical impulses. Some TENS units can be worn, others are free-standing. It does not hurt, but may cause tingling. TENS is particularly helpful for treating localised pain.

☐ **Copper bracelets.** One research study suggests that by wearing a copper bracelet, minute amounts of copper transfer through the skin, relieving pain and stiffness. These claims are controversial.

☐ **Relaxation therapy.** Relaxation calms mind and body and releases tension in your muscles, so relieving pain. You need a quiet place and 20 minutes to yourself. Play some music or listen to natural sounds like water. Find a comfortable position, breathe deeply, think tranquil thoughts and imagine pleasant scenes. You feel calm, refreshed and with a renewed sense of well-being. Other forms of relaxation involve guided imagery or **Visualisation.** A voice on tape guides you through a beautiful scene.

☐ **Meditation.** Some say meditation makes them feel refreshed and revitalised. It quietens the mind and lessens stress, thus reducing pain. You can meditate with a mantra, by focusing on breathing, or by concentrating on a small object like a flower. Some people find **Prayer** relaxing and comforting.

☐ **Hypnosis.** Hypnosis can soothe pain by creating a state of deep relaxation so that you can accept suggestions for positive change.

☐ **Sleep.** A good night's sleep restores energy and increases your ability to manage pain. It also gives your joints a chance to rest. Make sure that you go to bed at about the same time every night and invest in a comfortable bed.

☐ **Acupuncture and acupressure.** Needles or pressure are

placed at particular points, stimulating deep sensory nerves that tell the brain to release pain-killing endorphins.

☐ **Aromatherapy.** Essential oils are used with massage to calm and soothe: rosemary, benzoin, German camomile, camphor, juniper or lavender do this. Cypress, fennel, lemon and wintergreen detoxify and may reduce inflammation.

☐ **Nutritional therapy.** Supplements containing substances called flavonoids, pancreatic enzymes and bromelain, an enzyme found in pineapple, have anti-inflammatory properties, thus reducing pain.

(*See also Part III*)

AIDS AND GADGETS

No matter how badly your arthritis affects you, there is an aid, gadget or piece of equipment that can make your life easier. The range is vast and they are easier to obtain than ever – you can buy many gadgets in high street stores or through specialist mail order catalogues. (*See Useful Addresses at the end of the book for a range of suppliers.* The Disabled Living Foundation on 020 7289 6111 may be able to help you locate the product you want.)

Before paying for larger items, seek the advice of an occupational therapist from the Social Services department of your local council. They visit your home, advise on what aids and equipment you need, and show you how to use them. Some, for example, grab rails, are provided free of charge. For costlier items, such as stairlifts, you will be means-tested. You can sometimes borrow equipment from the Social Services department or your local hospital.

HELP FROM SOCIAL SERVICES

If you are impaired by arthritis, you may be able to get help from Social Services. Your general practitioner will need to tell the Social Services how your disability affects you. Arrange for an assessment from both an occupational therapist and a social worker. An occupational therapist will assess you for aids and equipment, and advise what is most suitable in your case. A social worker will assess you to see what Care Package you need. This may involve visits from a care assistant who can undertake basic housework, food preparation, and shopping. You may also be eligible for Meals on Wheels.

If your home needs to be adapted, this is done on the recommendation of the occupational therapist. For costly structural alterations, you may be eligible for a Disabled Facilities Grant, which is means-tested.

GADGETS FOR DAILY ACTIVITIES IN THE HOME

- ☐ **Reaching aid.** This is a long stick with tongs at the top. It helps you reach things without having to bend or stretch so that you can pick things up from the floor or grasp light objects from shelves and cupboards.
- ☐ **Plugs with handles.** If you find it difficult to grip plugs, try 'Handisocket' plugs with handles (from Keep Able Ltd on 08705 202122 (mail order), 01536 525153 (head office) or Independent Living Company on 020 8931 6000). These help you get a good grip. If existing sockets are too low for you, ask an electrician to move them higher up the wall, at your waist level, so that they are easier to reach.
- ☐ **Light switches.** If the light switches are too fiddly, have them replaced by large rocker-action switches. Or have an electrician install a pullcord in every room.
- ☐ **Thermostats.** It is possible to have a thermostat fitted that keeps the room at a constant temperature. This saves having to adjust knobs and dials.
- ☐ **Key holders and knob turners** can be attached to keys and knobs to give you a good, firm grip and longer leverage. Lever-type door handles are easier than knobs.
- ☐ **Tap turners** have long handles which give extra leverage and can be turned by using the back of the hand, elbow or wrist.
- ☐ **Long-handled dustpan and brush** and other long-handled, lightweight cleaning aids make housework easier.
- ☐ **Put a basket below the letter box** so that you do not have to bend down to pick up mail.

KITCHEN EQUIPMENT

Special equipment and gadgets can save you time and energy.

☐ **Perching stools** enable you to sit down when working.

☐ **Kettle tippers** help you avoid lifting hot, heavy teapots and kettles.

☐ **Opening jars and tins.** There are several devices. The 'Undoit' fixes under a shelf and enables you to turn a lid with both hands. The 'Twister' is a rubber cap that you place over the lid to increase your grip while turning. The similar 'Dycem' also works for yoghurt pots and large jars. The 'Fixit Workstation' helps keep jars and bottles stable so that you can open them more easily. The 'Dycem Mat' stops them slipping. With tin-openers, choose one that frees both your hands to turn the handle. An electric tin-opener will do the job for you.

☐ **Saucepans and cooking pots** should have a handle at both sides as they are easier to carry. Use a chip basket inside any saucepan for your vegetables to make draining easier and safer.

☐ **Labour-saving machines.** An electric food processor, automatic washing machine, drying machine and dishwasher can make your life much easier.

☐ **Kitchen utensils.** Spike boards hold food steady and leave your hands free. Hooped potato peelers are easy on the wrist. Mixing bowls can be kept steady on anti-slip mats, or buy one with suction pads.

☐ **Trolley.** Use a trolley rather than carry heavy trays.

EATING AND DRINKING

☐ **Two-handed mugs** make drinking easier and safer.

☐ **Easy-grip cutlery.** Large items are easier to grip. Lightweight cutlery is less of a strain on wrists and fingers.

BATHROOMS AND TOILETS

☐ **Toilets.** A raised toilet seat is useful for stiff knees and hips. Grab rails placed at the side of the toilet make it easier to get on and off. There are also free-standing toilet frames.

☐ **Commodes** can be placed by the bed so that you do not have to go to the bathroom. Portable urinals, male and female versions, can be used while lying in bed or sitting on the edge.

☐ **Bath aids.** If you find it difficult getting in and out of the bath, there are several aids available. Some are very cheap and low-tech, others are more high-tech and costly.

A small step by the bath means you do not have to lift your legs so high.

Non-slip bath mats that adhere to the bottom of the bath stop you slipping when you are standing up.

Grab rails help you step out of the bath.

A bath board and seat help you step in and out, but not to sit right down in the bath.

Mechanical bath lifts and hoists make it possible to have a bath independently. There are various types: The 'Mangar' is raised by compressed air and lowers when the valve is released. Another type is a hoist outside the bath with a swivel seat alongside it. They can be electrically powered or have a hand-winding operation, which may need a helper.

☐ **Shower aids.** Taking a shower can be easier if you have a shower seat. Some firms specialise in showers designed for disabled people.

☐ **Bathroom accessories.** Life can be made easier with a 'Flannel Strap', long-handled sponge, long-handled comb, electric toothbrush.

EQUIPMENT FOR GETTING AROUND THE HOUSE

☐ **Walking aids.** These include walking sticks, elbow crutches, and walking frames.

☐ **Stairlifts.** Stairlifts enable you to glide up and down stairs so that you do not need to struggle or have a downstairs room converted into a bedroom and bathroom. There are several stairlifts on the market to suit most stairs, and you can try some of them out at a Disabled Living Centre. Stairlifts can cost several thousand pounds. You may be able to get help towards the cost by getting a Disabled Facilities Grant through your local council. Ask your occupational therapist for advice.

☐ **Grab rails** on both sides of steps make them easier. If you cannot manage steps, you may need a ramp. If you can manage stairs but yours are too steep, half-steps may help.

☐ **Through-floor-lift.** If you cannot manage steps at all, even with a stairlift, this is an expensive alternative. You may be able to obtain a Disabled Facilities Grant to help pay for it.

☐ **Wheelchair.** A wheelchair needs plenty of space to move between rooms and turn around. You may need to make alterations to your home, such as wider doorways or ramps.

FURNITURE

☐ **Chairs.** For comfort and support, chairs should have a firm back and armrests. Low chairs can be difficult to get out of and do not give good support. You can raise the height of low chairs by putting blocks under the legs. 'Riser' chairs have an electrically-operated mechanism to help you on to your feet. The 'Backfriend' and similar devices can be added to chairs to give you firm support. Seek the advice of your occupational therapist and try some out before spending a lot of money.

☐ **Beds** should be the right height as a low bed can be hard to get out of. The mattress should be firm enough to support your spine without sagging.

If getting out of bed is a problem, there are some low-tech solutions such as a 'monkey pole' suspended over the bed head which you can grab, or a rope ladder attached to the foot of the bed. A device that looks like a bellows, called a Mattress Variator, fits under the mattress and sits you up at the push of a button. A Leglifter helps lift weak or painful legs into bed. Adjustable beds enable you to choose the most comfortable position just by the touch of a button. You can be in the head-up position, or the foot-up, or both. Twin beds have dual controls, so that each partner has the freedom to be in the position they want. This system can help relieve arthritic pain and give you a good night's sleep.

UTILITY COMPANIES

☐ **Gas and electric cookers and appliances.** Gas and electricity companies have a range of equipment and adaptations suitable for disabled people, such as large control knobs on hobs and cookers. Choose an oven at a convenient height. A microwave oven can be useful as they are easy to keep clean and the containers are lightweight.

☐ **Telephones.** BT make push-button telephones with extra large buttons. A cordless phone is useful. BT has a catalogue of equipment for disabled people: *The BT Guide for Disabled People*. Extension cords and sockets and an answering machine also make life easier.

DRESSING

☐ **Clothes.** Tips for getting dressed more easily: sew on bigger buttons or enlarge button holes; add a large ring to zip tabs; use a front-fastening bra. The 'Snappy Dresser' helps you get a coat on and off with little shoulder movement. Consider wearing trousers with elasticised waists so that you can just pull them on and off. A simple dressing stick with a hook at one end and a rubber at the other is useful for helping to get clothes on.

☐ **Shoes.** Wear comfortable, well-fitting shoes that do not put abnormal strain on the joints of your feet. Some shoes have Velcro fastenings – easier to do up than laces.

HOBBIES

Tips include:

☐ A heavy book on a tilted cantilever table on castors, or use a bookrest.

☐ Writing paper can be held in place by a magnetic board.

☐ Electric typewriters, word processors or computers are easier to write with than pens.

☐ A card holder makes it possible to play cards without holding them.

- ☐ 'Stirex' scissors have a spring-loaded action, making them easier to use.
- ☐ Battery-operated scissors make any craftwork easier.
- ☐ A needle holder makes knitting easier; or try using a knitting machine.

GARDENING

Pain in the joints may make gardening difficult, but there are many ways to overcome this. You can use different gardening methods, change the design of your garden, and use tools that make gardening easier. Be careful not to crouch too much as this bends the knees to the extreme, and overdoing things can lead to flare-ups. Change your position frequently by changing jobs, and do a little amount often. Think about how you move, and keep warm.

Helpful gadgets for the garden include:

- ☐ A kneeling stool which allows you to bend forward with your spine straight.
- ☐ Long-handled tools help you do work without bending.
- ☐ Tools should be lightweight.

GETTING OUT AND ABOUT

With so many mobility aids available, there is no need to be trapped in your own home.

Seek professional advice from an occupational therapist or physiotherapist before buying any walking or mobility aids as it is easy to choose something that may not be suitable for your particular needs.

- ☐ **Walking aids** need to be the right height for you. Aids include walking frames with a shopping basket, four-wheeled shopping trolleys, for example, 'The Sholley', 'Shop-a-seat' or 'Chairman' – a combined shopping trolley and seat so that you can rest when you want.
- ☐ **Wheelchairs** are useful if you find walking too difficult. You may be able to get a manual wheelchair via your doctor from your District Wheelchair Service or through your local health

authority. Alternatively, for a list of wheelchair services, try the Net with www.kcl.ac.uk. Electric wheelchairs and scooters do not need to be pushed or self-propelled, giving you more independence.

☐ **Shopping.** There are many supermarkets where someone will help you with packing and loading. If shopping is too much for you, care assistants from the Social Services may be able to do it for you. Nowadays, you can buy virtually anything from mail order catalogues or through the Internet.

☐ **Cars** give you freedom. When buying a car, make sure you can get in and out easily. Swivel seats can help. Back supports can make driving more comfortable. Heated back supports are ideal. It is easier to drive a car with power-assisted steering, electric windows, and automatic gears. There are firms specialising in adaptations if you need hand controls. It is worth joining a disabled drivers' organisation.

The motability scheme

If you get the Mobility Component of Disability Living Allowance, you should be able to get a car through the Motability Scheme, which is cheaper and easier than buying a car yourself and takes much of the worry out of owning a car. You have the choice of leasing a car for three years, or buying one outright. The advantage of leasing is that you always have the peace of mind of driving a relatively new car. All you pay is a deposit (some cars require no deposit). The Mobility Component of your Disability Living Allowance is paid directly to Motability Finance Ltd to pay for the leasing. Insurance and servicing are included in the price. At the end of three years, you trade your car in for a new one. (Motability: 01279 635666.)

Dial-a-ride and mobility schemes

If you cannot drive and there is no one to drive you, find out about mobility schemes from your local council. There are often mini buses that will take disabled people to and from where they need to go.

Useful addresses

HELP AND SUPPORT GROUPS

Arthritis Research Campaign (ARC), formerly The Arthritis and Rheumatism Council for Research
P.O. Box 177
Chesterfield
Derbyshire
S41 7TQ
01246 558033

Arthritis Care
18 Stephenson Way
London
NW1 2HD
020 7916 1500
Helpline: 0808 800 4050
Young Arthritis Care: 0808 808 2000

Association for Dance Movement Therapy
c/o The Art Therapies Department
Springfield Hospital
Glenburnie Road
London
SW17 7DJ
020 8682 6237

The Association of Reflexologists
27 Old Gloucester Street
London
WC1N 3XX
08705 673320

Bach Centre
Mount Vernon
Sotwell
Wallingford
Oxfordshire
OX10 0PZ
01491 834678

Back Care (formerly known as Back Pain Association)
16 Elmtree Road
Teddington
Middlesex
TW11 8ST
020 8977 5474

British Acupuncture Council
63 Jeddo Road
London
W12 9HQ
020 8735 0400

**British Association of
Occupational Therapists**
106-114 Borough High Street
London
SE1 1LB
020 7357 6480

**British Association of
Psychotherapy**
37 Mapesbury Road
London
NW2 4HJ
020 8452 9823

British Chiropractic Association
Blagrave House
17 Blagrave Street
Reading
Berkshire
RG1 1QB
020 8950 5950

British Hypnotherapy Association
67 Upper Berkeley Street
London
W1H 7QX
020 7723 4443

**British Federation of Massage
Practitioners**
Greenbank House
65a Adelphi Street
Preston
PR1 7BH
01772 881063

**British Sjögren's Syndrome
Association**
Unit 1
Manor Workshop
West End
Nailsea
Bristol
BS48 4WD
01275 854215

British Wheel of Yoga
25 Jermyn Street
Sleaford
Lincolnshire
NG34 7RU
01529 306851

**Centre for Accessible
Environment**
Nutmeg House
60 Gainsford Street
London
SE1 2NY
020 7357 8182

Disabled Drivers' Association
Central Office
Ashwellthorpe
Norwich
NR16 1EX
01508 489449

Disabled Living Foundation
380-384 Harrow Road
London
W9 2HU
020 7289 6111

General Council and Register of Naturopaths
Goswell House
2 Goswell Road
Street
BA16 0JG
01458 840072

The General Osteopathic Council
176 Tower Bridge Road
London
SE1 3LU
020 7357 6655

Institute for Complementary Medicine
PO Box 194
London
SE16 7QZ
020 7237 5165

The International Federation of Aromatherapists
182 Chiswick High Road
London
W4 1WP
020 8742 2605

The Iyengar Yoga Institute
223a Randolph Avenue
London
W9 1NL
020 7624 3080

Lupus UK
St James House
Eastern Road
Romford
Essex
RM1 3NH
01708 731251

The Mobility Information Service
Unit B1
Greenwood Court
Cartmel Drive
Harlescott
Shrewsbury
Shropshire
SY1 3TB
01743 463072

Motability
Goodman House
Station Approach
Harlow
Essex
CM20 2ET
01279 635666

National Ankylosing Spondylitis Society
PO Box 179
Mayfield
East Sussex
TN20 6ZL
01435 873527

The National Institute of Medical Herbalists
56 Longbrook Street
Exeter
EX4 6AH
01392 426022

National Osteoporosis Society
Camerton
Bath
BA2 0PJ
01761 471771

The Psoriasis Association
7 Milton Street
Northampton
NN2 7JG
01604 711129

The Royal Association for Disability and Rehabilitation
12 City Forum
250 City Road
London
EC1V 8AF
020 7250 3222

School of Meditation
158 Holland Park Avenue
London
W11 4UH
020 7603 6116

School of T'ai Chi Ch'uan Centre for Healing
07626 914540

Society of Teachers of the Alexander Technique
129 Camden Mews
London
NW1 9AH
020 7284 3338

Transcendental Meditation
Freepost
London
SW1P 4YY
08705 143733

The Yoga Therapy Centre
Royal London Homeopathic
Hospital Trust
60 Great Ormond Street
London
WC1N 3HR
020 7419 7195

RETAIL OUTLETS AND MAIL ORDER

The Back Shop
14 New Cavendish Street
London
W1M 7LJ
020 7935 9120

Damart
Bowling Green Mills
Bingley
West Yorkshire
BD16 3ZD
01274 510000

Days Medical Aids Ltd
Litchard Industrial Estate
Bridgend
Mid Glamorgan
CF31 2AL
01656 657495

Disabled Drivers Motor Club Ltd
(DDMC)
Cottingham Way
Thrapstone
Northamptonshire
NN14 4PL
01832 734724

Helping Hands Co (Ledbury) Ltd
Bromyard Trading Estate
Ledbury
Hertfordshire
HR8 1NS
01531 635678

Independent Living Company
11 Hale Lane
Mill Hill
London
NW7 3NU
020 8931 6000

John Bell & Croyden Chemists
52-54 Wigmore Street
London
W1H 0AU
020 7935 5555

Keep Able Ltd
38c Telford Way
Telford Way Industrial Estate
Kettering
Northants
NN16 8UN
01536 525153
Mail order: 08705 202122

Nottingham Rehab Supplies Ltd
Findel House
Excelsior Rd
Ashby de la Zouche
Leicestershire
LE65 1NG
01159 452345

For list of wheelchair services, www.kcl.ac.uk

"Vinegar

Nature's secret weapon"
by Maxwell Stein

You'll find vinegar in just about every kitchen in the country – but most of us only ever use it on chips or as a salad dressing. Did you know there are hundreds of other uses for vinegar? In his incredible new book, Maxwell Stein looks at how vinegar has been used around the home and as a traditional remedy. If you thought vinegar was just used for salad dressing... then you're in for a big surprise!

"Vinegar – nature's secret weapon" is a new book in which the author looks at over 325 tried and tested uses for vinegar. For example, Maxwell checks out how vinegar has been used to:
- Polish the chrome on the car
- Clean work surfaces, mirrors and glass
- Repair scratches in wood
- Whiten whites, brighten colours and fade sweat stains
- Ease the pain of insect bites
- Lift stains on carpets
- Remove ink stains
- Clean brass, copper and pewter
- Banish unpleasant odours
- Dissolve chewing gum
- And much, much more.

Maxwell also tells us why he thinks vinegar can be used to:
- Soothe tired and aching feet
- Relieve headaches
- Lift painful corns and calluses
- Clear embarrassing dandruff
- Help treat burns

- Help fade age spots
- Prevent infections
- Ease nausea and stomach upset
- Relieve coughs and tickly throats
- Cure hiccups – fast
- Relieve a sore throat
- Guard against food poisoning
- Disinfect almost anything – it's used in many hospitals
- Soothe painful sunburn

Over 325 different uses in total. But that's not all, Maxwell also covers Honey and Garlic and tells you why he believes they are both powerful natural allies of vinegar.

Honey and Garlic too!

As a special bonus and for a limited time only, we have included two completely free sections to the Vinegar book – so, not only do you get a Vinegar book, but you also get a Honey book and Garlic book too – that's three of nature's secret wonders all for just £9.95.

You'll see how Maxwell put these three natural wonders to the test as he looks at many common ailments. He talks about how honey and garlic have been used as simple, yet cost effective home remedies – alone or mixed with vinegar <u>and</u> at a fraction of what you'd pay for commercially prepared products.

In these two special BONUS sections of *"Vinegar, – nature's secret weapon"*, Maxwell looks at many health problems and whether simple treatments can be used to tackle them, such as:

- An easy poultice which has been used to treat painful joints
- A simple drink used to ease muscle pain fast!

- An easy to prepare mixture to prevent burns from scarring
- A tasty recipe, used to help keep cholesterol at a healthy level
- A fast remedy used to treat cold sores
- A morning treat to ease the discomfort of asthma
- An ancient Indian broth, used for blood pressure
- Delicious tea used to add sparkle to dull sex lives
- A tasty brew that has been used to help lose weight
- A method used to stop toothache by relieving pain naturally
- A Russian folk remedy, used to treat colds
- A fast method for clearing spots and blemishes
- A simple method to ease gas and indigestion problems fast
- A preparation which has been used to combat the flu

And many, many more health questions answered.

These special bonus sections on Honey & Garlic are only available for a limited time, so to avoid disappointment, please send your order now – and you'll be getting three for the price of one. All with a full, three month money back guarantee.

To Order

Call our freephone orderline on **08000 270527** or send your payment of £9.95 plus £1.95 p&p (payable to Windsor Health) or credit/debit card details including your card number, start date, expiry date and issue number for Switch together with your name, address and book title to:

**Windsor Health,
Dept RT1,
36 Stephenson Road,
Totton,
Southampton
SO40 3YD**

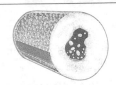

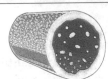